Crossway Bible Guide

Series editors: Ian Coffey (NT), Stephen Gaukroger (OT)
Old Testament editor: Stephen Dray
New Testament editor: Steve Motyer

Titles in this series

Genesis, Richard and Tricia Johnson
Exodus, Stephen Dray
Leviticus, Derek Tidball
Joshua, Charles Price
Ruth and Esther, Debra Reid
Ezra and Nehemiah, Dave Cave
Psalms 1 – 72, Alan Palmer
Psalms 73 – 150, Alan Palmer and Debra Reid
Isaiah, Philip Hacking
Six Minor Prophets, Michael Wilcock
Haggai, Zechariah and Malachi, John James
Matthew's Gospel, Stephen Dray
Mark's Gospel, David Hewitt
Luke's Gospel, Simon Jones
John's Gospel, Ian Barclay
Acts, Stephen Gaukroger
Romans, David Coffey
1 Corinthians, Robin Dowling and Stephen Dray
2 Corinthians, Jonathan Lamb
Ephesians, Steve Motyer
Philippians, Ian Coffey
Colossians and Philemon, Stephen Gaukroger and
    Derek Wood
1 & 2 Thessalonians, Alec Motyer and Steve Motyer
Timothy and Titus, Michael Griffiths
James, David Field
1 Peter, Andrew Whitman
1, 2, 3 John, Diane Tidball

The Bible with Pleasure, Steve Motyer
Discovering the New Testament, Simon Jones
Housegroups: The Leaders' Survival Guide, Ian Coffey and
    Stephen Gaukroger (eds.)
Rebuild, Fran Beckett (ed.)

Joshua: Crossway Bible Guide

Charles Price

Crossway Books, Leicester

CROSSWAY BOOKS
Norton Street, Nottingham, NG7 3 HR, England
Email: ivp@uccf.org.uk
Website: www.ivpbooks.com

First edition 1993
Second edition 1997

This edition first published 1997
Reprinted 2009

British Library Cataloguing in Publication Data

A catalogue record for this book is available from
the British Library

ISBN 1–85684–164–2

Set in Palatino

Typeset in Great Britain by Parker Typesetting Service, Leicester
Printed in Great Britain by Ashford Colour Press Ltd, Gosport, Hants

CONTENTS

Welcome!   8
How to use this Bible Guide   9
How to tackle personal Bible study   9
How to tackle your group Bible study   10
How to tackle *Joshua*   13
What can we expect to learn from *Joshua?*   14
Finding your way round this book   15

1 Viewing the land   17
Canaan before the book of Joshua   19
Joshua before the book of Joshua   22

2 Entering the land – Joshua 1–4   27
The dawn of a new era – Joshua succeeds
Moses   1:1–5   29
The borders of Israel   32
Joshua instructed in principles of success   1:6–9   33
Preparing to enter Canaan   1:10–15   36
The people affirm loyalty to Joshua   1:16–18   39
Spies in the house of Rahab   2:1–7   41
Rahab believes in Israel's victory   2:8–24   44
The scarlet cord   45
Preparing to cross the Jordan   3:1–13   46
The ark of the covenant   48
.Crossing the Jordan   3:14–17   50
The miracle of the Jordan   51
Collecting twelve stones   4:1–18   52

The Red Sea and the Jordan   4:19–24   55

3 Conquering the land – Joshua 5–12   59
Circumcision at Gilgal   5:1–9   61
   Circumcision   63
The passover and the end of manna   5:10–12   64
The commander of the army of the LORD   5:13–15   66
   Theophany   68
Preparing to conquer Jericho   6:1–5   70
Seven days around the city   6:6–27   72
   The killing of seemingly innocent people   75
The sin of Achan   7:1–9   76
The sentence of God   7:10–26   79
   Making decisions Old Testament-style   82
The destruction of Ai   8:1–29   83
The renewal of the covenant   8:30–35   86
The Gibeonite confidence trick   9:1–15   89
The deception exposed   9:16–27   92
The coalition of Amorite kings   10:1–5   94
Victory is the Lord's   10:6–15   97
The southern cities conquered   10:16–43   101
The confederation of northern kings   11:1–5   103
The battle is the Lord's   11:6–15   106
   Hazor   108
Joshua conquers the land   11:16–23   109
Summary of the conquest   12:1–24   112
   The Philistines   115

4 Occupying the land – Joshua 13–22   117
Land still to be taken   13:1–7   119
The inheritance of the tribes east of Jordan   13:8–14   122
Details of land for Reuben, Gad and the half-tribe
of Manasseh   13:15–33   125
Dividing up the land west of Jordan   14:1–5   127
Caleb – the strong man at eighty-five   14:6–15   130
The inheritance of Judah   15:1–63   133

The inheritance of the children of Joseph   16:1–10   137
The five daughters of Zelophehad   17:1–6   138
The boundaries of Manasseh   17:7–18   141
Setting up the tabernacle   18:1   144
    The tabernacle   146
Survey of the land   18:2–28   147
Inheritances of Simeon, Zebulun, Issachar, Asher,
Naphtali, Dan and the personal inheritance
of Joshua   19:1–51   149
Cities of refuge   20:1–9   152
Towns for the Levites   21:1–45   156
The eastern tribes go home   22:1–5   159
The altar built at Jordan   22:6–34   162

5 Preserving the land – Joshua 23–24   165
Looking back in gratitude   23:1–5   167
Looking forward in confidence   23:6–16   170
A review of God's goodness   24:1–13   173
Facing the issues   24:14–15   177
Renewing the covenant   24:16–28   179
Three funerals   24:29–33   182

Further reading   184

Maps
1 The conquest of Canaan   100
2 The tribal divisions of Canaan   128
3 Cities of refuge   155

Welcome!

These days, meeting together to study the Bible appears to be a booming leisure-time activity in many parts of the world. In the United Kingdom alone, it is estimated that over one million people each week meet in home Bible-study groups.

This series has been designed to help such groups and, in particular, those who lead them, but they are also eminently suitable for individual study. We are also aware of the needs of those who preach and teach to larger groups as well as the hard-pressed student, all of whom often look for a commentary that gives a concise summary and lively application of a particular passage.

We have therefore enlisted authors who are in the business of teaching the Bible to others and are doing it well. They have kept in their sights two clear aims:

1. To explain and apply the message of the Bible in non-technical language.
2. To encourage discussion, prayer and action on what the Bible teaches.

All of us engaged in the project believe that the Bible is the Word of God – given to us in order that people might discover him and his purposes for our lives. We believe that the sixty-six books which go to make up the Bible, although written by different people, in different places, at different times, through different circumstances, have a single unifying theme: that theme is Salvation. This means free forgiveness and the removal of all our guilt, it means the gift of eternal life and it means the wholeness of purpose and joy which God has designed us to experience here and now, all of this being made possible through the Lord Jesus Christ.

How to use this Bible Guide

These guides have been prepared both for personal study and for the leaders and members of small groups. More information about group study follows on the next few pages.

You can use this book very profitably as a personal study guide. The short studies are ideal for daily reading: the first of the following questions is usually aimed to help you with personal reflection (see *How to tackle personal Bible study*). If you prefer to settle down to a longer period of study you can use groups of three to five studies, and thus get a better overview of a longer Bible passage. In either case using the Bible Guide will help you to be disciplined about regular study, a habit that countless Christians have found greatly beneficial. (See also *How to tackle Joshua* for methods of selecting studies if you do not intend to use them all.)

Yet a third use for these Bible Guides is as a quarry for ideas for the busy Bible teacher, providing outlines and application for those giving talks or sermons or teaching children. You will need more than this book can offer of course, but the way the Bible text is broken down, comments offered and questions raised may well suggest directions to follow.

How to tackle personal Bible study

We have already suggested that you might use this book as a personal study guide. Now for some more detail.

One of the best methods of Bible study is to read the text through carefully several times, possibly using different versions or translations. Having reflected on the material it is a good discipline to write down your own thoughts before doing anything else. At this stage the introduction of other books can be useful. If you are using this book as your main study resource, then read through the relevant sections carefully, turning up the Bible references that are mentioned. The questions at the end of each chapter are specifically designed to help you to apply the passage to your own situation. You may find it helpful to write your answers to the questions in your notes.

It is a good habit to conclude with prayer, bringing before God the things you have learned.

If this kind of in-depth study is too demanding for you and you have only a short time at your disposal, read the Bible passage, read the comments in the Bible Guide, think round one of the questions and commit what you have learned to God in a brief prayer. This would take about fifteen minutes without rushing it.

How to tackle your group Bible study

1. Getting help

If you are new to leading groups you will obviously want to get all the help you can from ministers and experienced friends. Books are also extremely helpful and we strongly recommend a book prepared by the editors of this series of Bible Guides: *Housegroups: the leaders' survival guide*: edited by Ian Coffey and Stephen Gaukroger (Crossway Books, 1996). This book looks at the whole range of different types of group, asking what is the point of it all, what makes a good leader, how to tackle your meeting, how to help the members, how to study, pray, share, worship and plenty of other pointers, tips and guidelines.

This book is a 'must' for all leaders of small groups. It is written by a team of people widely experienced in this area. It is available at your local Christian bookshop. If you have difficulty in obtaining a copy write to Crossway Books, Norton Street, Nottingham, NG7 3HR, UK.

2. Planning a programme with your Bible Guide

This guide is a commentary on God's word, written to help a group to get the most out of their studies. Although it is never ideal to chop up Scripture into small pieces, which the authors never intended, huge chunks are indigestible and we have tried to provide a diet of bite-sized mouthfuls.

The book is divided into parts, indicated by a title and a large number. If you want to get an overview of the Bible book in a series of meetings you will need to take one or more parts for each meeting. Read them yourself first and prepare a short summary of the part(s) you are tackling for your group. Ideally you could write it on a sheet of A5 paper and hand a copy to each member.

Then choose one study from the part you are dealing with as a basis for your meeting. Do not attempt to pack more than one study into one meeting but choose the crucial one, the study which best crystallizes the message. There are examples in *How to tackle Joshua* below.

If you do not intend to cover the whole Bible book, choose a series of studies to suit the number of meetings you have available. Each part of the commentary is divided into a few (usually 3–5) studies. If you have an eight-week programme with weekly meetings you could aim to cover two parts of the book. It is a good idea to use consecutive studies, not to dodge about. You will then build up a detailed picture of one section of Scripture. Alternative examples of programmes of study for this book are given in *How to tackle Joshua*.

3. Resources

You will find any or all of these books of great value in providing background to your Bible knowledge. Put some of them on your Christmas list and build up your library.

New Bible Dictionary or *New Concise Bible Dictionary* (IVP)
New Bible Atlas (IVP)

New Bible Commentary (21st Century edition) (IVP)
Everyday Life in Bible Times: John Thompson (IVP)
The Bible User's Manual (IVP)
The Lion Handbook to the Bible (Lion Publishing)
The Message of the Bible (Lion Publishing)
NIV Study Bible (Hodder & Stoughton)
The Bible with Pleasure: Stephen Motyer (Crossway Books)

The relevant volume in the IVP Tyndale Commentary series will give you reliable and detailed help with any knotty points you may encounter.

4. Preparing to lead

Reading, discussing with friends, studying, praying, reflecting on life . . . preparation can be endless. But do not be daunted by that. If you wait to become the perfect leader you will never start at all. The really vital elements in preparation are:

▶ prayer (not only in words but an attitude of dependence on God, 'Lord, I can't manage this on my own')

▶ familiarity with the study passage (careful reading of the text, the Bible Guide study and any other resource books that throw light on it) and

▶ a clear idea of where you hope to get in the meeting (notes on your introduction, perhaps, recap what was covered at the last meeting, and what direction you hope the questions will take you in – don't force the group to give your answers).

Here is a short checklist for the busy group leader:

Have I prayed about the meeting?
Have I decided exactly what I want to achieve through the meeting?
Have I prepared the material?
Am I clear about the questions that will encourage positive group discussion?

Am I gently encouraging silent members?

Am I, again gently, quietening the chatterers?

Am I willing to admit ignorance?

Am I willing to listen to what the group says and to value their contributions?

Am I ready not to be dogmatic, not imposing my ideas on the group?

Have I planned how to involve the group in discovering for themselves?

Have I developed several 'prayer points' that will help focus the group?

Are we applying Scripture to our experience of real life or only using it as a peg to hang our opinions on?

Are we finding resources for action and change or just having a nice talk?

Are we all enjoying the experience together?

How to tackle *Joshua*

Now let's assume you are planning an eight-week course of studies (you will have to make the adjustments if you have more or fewer meetings). Where do you begin? This is entirely up to you and your group of course but, to get you started, here are a few possible routes you might take:

1. A bird's eye view of the story

1:1–5	5:1–9	10:1–5	20:1–9
3:14–17	6:1–5	12:1–24	24:1–13

2. A character sketch of Joshua

1:6–9	8:30–35	11:16–23	23:6–16
1:16–18	10:6–15	13:1–7	24:16–28

3. Learning to be strong in a crisis

1:10–15	3:1–13	8:1–29	23:6–16
2:1–7	5:13–15	10:6–15	24:14–15

4. Building faith in God

2:8–24	7:1–26 (two studies)	14:6–15	20:1–9
4:1–18	11:6–15	17:1–6	23:1–5

These outlines are meant to be springboards for your own ideas, so please do not follow them slavishly. Adapt them for your own use, merge them or ignore them. In any case much of Joshua will go unread if you concentrate only on these short snippets. You as leader will need to read carefully the whole book so that you can refer your group to sections they have not read. It would be wise to read a whole chapter when studying a part of it – the context often throws light on the verses you are looking at.

What can we expect to learn from *Joshua*?

Whilst being our key source of information about Israel's occupation of the land of Canaan, it would be a mistake to regard the value of this book as only historical. *Joshua* is primarily a book about God working out his purposes in the cut and thrust of real-life situations. We will discover:

▶ The source of boldness in intimidating circumstances.

▶ How human weakness provides the opportunity for God to demonstrate his strength.

▶ How to deal with disappointment.

▶ How to find restoration after failure.

▶ Why I cannot fully trust in God without a corresponding obedience to God.

▶ Why reminders of God's power in the past can instil confidence in his power for the present.

▶ How the principles of God's working in the Old Testament are his principles of operating in the present.

Finding your way round this book

In our Bible Guides we have developed special symbols to make things easier to follow. Every study therefore has an opening section which is the passage in a nutshell.

The main section is the one that *makes sense of the passage*.

Questions

Every passage also has special questions for personal and group study after the main section. Some questions are addressed to us as individuals, some speak to us as members of our church or home group, while others concern us as members of God's people worldwide. The questions are deliberately designed:

▶ to get people thinking about the passage

▶ to apply the text to 'real life' situations

▶ to encourage reflection, discussion and action!

As a group leader you may well discover additional questions that will have special relevance to your group, so look out for these and note them in your preparation time.

Digging deeper

Some passages, however, require an extra amount of explanation, and we have put these sections into two categories. The first kind gives additional background material that helps us to understand something factual. For example, if we dig deeper into the gospels, it helps us to know who the Pharisees were, so that we can see more easily why they related to Jesus in the way they did. These background sections are marked with a spade.

Important doctrines

The second kind of explanatory section appears with passages which have important doctrines contained in them and which we need to study in more depth if we are to grow as Christians. Special sections that explain them to us in greater detail are marked with a face as above.

VIEWING THE LAND

Canaan before the book of Joshua

Joshua is a book about God in action. The dramatic events recorded in its pages have only one satisfactory explanation: the same God who miraculously delivered Israel from slavery in Egypt forty years earlier, equally miraculously brought them in to the land of Canaan he had promised to them. This is not a record of what Joshua did for God so much as a record of what God did through Joshua. The principles that enable God to work in human experience are demonstrated and taught against the realistic background of conflict, failure and human frailty. While teaching the reality of warfare, Joshua reveals the possibility of victory. It teaches us that failure need never lead to despair but may become the springboard to a greater trust and confidence in God.

The historical events recorded in the book of Joshua are important to our understanding of the history of Israel, but Joshua is telling another story alongside that. He is telling the story of how ordinary people like you and me may know the victory of God in their lives and circumstances. To fully appreciate the text of Joshua we must first understand the events in Israel's history that made necessary the invasion of Canaan by Israel.

The story of the book of Joshua begins neither in Joshua nor at the Jordan river, but more than 500 years earlier with Abraham in Ur. When Abraham arrived in Canaan he came to the site of the great tree of Moreh at Shechem. There the Lord appeared to him and said, 'To your offspring I will give this land' (Genesis 12:7). That promise was not properly realized for over five centuries, and the book of Joshua records the descendants of Abraham at last occupying the land that had been promised so long before. The covenant God made involved three specific clauses which were to be repeated and reaffirmed at various points through Israel's history.

1. Property – the land

'The LORD had said to Abram, "Leave your country, your people and your father's household and go to the land I will show you"' (Genesis 12:1). Abram left Ur of the Chaldeans, and travelled through the land to Canaan where 'The LORD appeared to him and said, "To your offspring I will give this land"' (Genesis 12:7). This particular piece of land was set apart by God as the property of this people.

2. People – the nation

'I will make you into a great nation . . . I will make your name great . . .' (Genesis 12:2). Abraham at this stage was married though childless. A nation would come from his body, and this nation would be the channel of God's particular plans on earth.

3. Prosperity – the blessing

'I will bless those who bless you, and whoever curses you I will curse; and all peoples on earth will be blessed through you' (Genesis 12:3). The nation would be protected by God, and caused to prosper.

It is important to note that God's setting aside of his group of people is ultimately for the interests of others. The people's self-realization should focus on its means of being a blessing to others rather than on a sense of elitism as God's chosen nation.

The land, the people and the promise of prosperity were intricately bound up. It was the people in the land that would enjoy the promise. The wrong people in the right land were not subject to the blessing – therefore much of Joshua deals with getting the wrong people out. Conversely the right people in the wrong land were not the subject of blessing, for they had been enslaved in Egypt, weakened in the desert and would later be punished in Babylon. The history of Israel is the history of keeping property, people and promise together. The story of Joshua is the story of getting the right people in to the right land.

Israel's stay in Egypt, culminating in slavery, lasted for 430 years. Then God intervened and brought them out of Egypt under the leadership of Moses, no longer a family but a nation of around 2 million people (Exodus 12:37; 38:26; there were 603,550 men over the age of 20 years, and wives and children would increase that number to approximately 2 million).

This background helps us to understand the message of Joshua. It is a record of God getting his people back to the place where they were supposed to be – the place where his covenant could be fully implemented – and they in turn would be the source of blessing to the world they were intended to be. The story of Joshua is not a story of God doing something new for his people so much as God getting the people back to where they were always intended to be.

As such this book beautifully parallels and portrays the Christian life. God created mankind in such a way that he can fully function as intended to only in reliance upon the life of God himself. In the fall man sinned and became 'separated from the life of God' (Ephesians 4:18), meaning he died spiritually, for spiritual life is the life of God. The intention of the work of Christ therefore is to put right what went wrong and to restore the life of God to human experience. Christ came not to do something new so much as to restore us to the original purpose of our existence and the original means by which we should function. To live under the Lordship of Christ and in dependency upon his Spirit is going to place us in conflict with 'the world, the flesh and the devil' (to quote Martin Luther). As God's people sought to reoccupy Canaan they discovered a battleground. Their experience will parallel for us so many aspects of Christian living and spiritual warfare.

Joshua before the book of Joshua

At the time of deliverance from Egypt Joshua was a young man (Exodus 33:11). He makes seven separate appearances in the wilderness narrative, all of which reveal strategic experience that prepared him for his coming responsibility.

Fighting the Amalekites (Exodus 17:8–16)

The first battle fought by Israel after leaving Egypt was against the Amalekites at Rephidim. Joshua's very first mention was his appointment by Moses to choose an army of men and then go and fight the Amalekites whilst Moses himself went to the top of the hill with the staff of God in his hands. As Moses raised his staff in the air, Joshua found himself winning the battle, but as Moses lowered his hands the Amalekites were winning the battle. When Moses grew tired Aaron and Hur sat him on a stone and, standing one on each side of him, held up his hands and Joshua consequently overcame the Amalekite army. Whatever else that story teaches, Joshua learned a lesson here that would be of immense significance to him in days to come: *victory against the enemies of God is not something to be won but something to be received!* This lesson was perhaps the most crucial for Joshua in preparing him subsequently to conquer Canaan.

On Mount Sinai (Exodus 24:13 – 31:18)

The initial giving of the law on Sinai was to Moses alone. Then God called Moses to go higher up the mountain and take only Joshua with him. God met them in a 'cloud of glory'. The detailed instructions for building the tabernacle were received on this occasion along with the elaborate rituals concerning the priesthood and the sacrificial system by which the people would have access to God. The second lesson of importance to his subsequent work was to be learned: *failure to meet God on his own terms is to meet him not as a friend but as a Judge!*

The golden calf (Exodus 32)

During the forty days Moses and Joshua were on Mount Sinai the Israelites, under Aaron's guidance, had melted down their gold jewelry and built a golden calf claiming, 'These are your gods, O Israel, who brought you up out of Egypt'. Hearing the celebration Joshua, with his soldier's ear, mistook it for 'the sound of war in the camp'. But the sound was of something worse than war, it was the sound of rebellion. When Moses saw what was happening he threw down the stone tablets of the law and smashed them. The young man Joshua was alongside Moses witnessing this event. The third lesson Joshua learned was that: *no-one can serve two masters and survive!*

In the tent of meeting (Exodus 33:11)

Moses pitched a tent outside the camp calling it the 'tent of meeting'. This was the prototype of the tabernacle where God would make his presence known in a pillar of cloud. Moses took Joshua with him into the tent and he was allowed to listen when 'The LORD would speak face to face as a man speaks with his friend'. The fourth lesson Joshua learned was: *communion with God is necessary for God's service!*

Prophesying in the camp (Numbers 11:24–30)

When two of the seventy elders were given the Spirit to prophesy in the camp (and not in the tabernacle with the other sixty-eight), Joshua tried to stop them. 'But Moses replied, "Are you jealous for my sake? I wish that all the LORD's people were prophets and that the LORD would put his Spirit on them!"' Joshua learns his fifth lesson: *God works through whom he will, sometimes outside of our expectations!* Joshua must not allow his own disappointment with people who apparently have disobeyed instructions to blind him to God's willingness to continue working through them. He is also learning that his perception of a case is not always right. God sees things differently!

Spying out Canaan (Numbers 13–14)

Joshua was one of the twelve men, representative of each tribe, who were sent on a 40-day secret exploration of Canaan from Kadesh Barnea. On their return the spies all reported how rich and fruitful the land was. Everything God had said about the prosperity of the land was true. But ten of the twelve reported a problem, 'The people who live there are powerful and the cities are fortified and very large.' They then listed some of the seven nations who inhabited the land claiming, 'We can't attack those people; they are stronger than we are', and they spread amongst the people a bad report. The other two spies, Joshua and Caleb, agreed the enemies were real but affirmed, 'If the LORD is pleased with us, he will lead us into that land, a land flowing with milk and honey, and will give it to us. . . . Their protection is gone, but the LORD is with us. Do not be afraid of them' (Numbers 14:8–9).

The ten spies won the argument and instead of advancing into Canaan as God had planned for them to do, the nation turned tail and spent the next 38 years wandering in the wilderness with the sentence of death over every adult male over 20 years at the time of leaving Egypt, with the exception of Joshua and Caleb. Every one of them had died and been buried in the wilderness before the Israelites would ever set foot in the promised land. Joshua and Caleb together had learned and tried to appropriate a fundamental principle of spiritual effectiveness: *Do not attempt merely what is possible, attempt what you believe to be right. It is God's business to make possible what is right!*

Joshua also learned through this incident that you do not make decisions on the basis of a majority opinion, but by ascertaining what God wants. As a democracy the interests of Israel would never rise above their own selfish and vested concerns, but as a theocracy (that is, God-governed) the issues would all relate to one central consideration: What is the will of God?

Being commissioned as leader (Numbers 27:12–22; Deuteronomy 3:28; 31:1–8)

The ordination of Joshua took place on the plain of Moab, east of the Jordan river, towards the end of the wilderness years. All the people sentenced to die in the wilderness had now done so and had been buried: 'not one of them was left except Caleb son of Jephunneh and Joshua son of Nun' (Numbers 26:65). Moses too has been forbidden to enter Canaan. He would climb a mountain in the Abarim range to see the land, but he would not lead them in. Instead he is to commission Joshua to lead the people in.

Four things were made available to Joshua that would enable him to lead the nation effectively:

1. 'The LORD said to Moses, "Take Joshua son of Nun, a man in whom is the Spirit, and lay your hand on him."' (Numbers 27:18)
2. 'But commission Joshua, and encourage and strengthen him, for he will lead this people across and will cause them to inherit the land that you will see.' (Deuteronomy 3:28)
3. 'Then Moses summoned Joshua and said to him in the presence of all Israel, "Be strong and courageous . . . The LORD himself goes before you and will be with you; he will never leave you nor forsake you."' (Deuteronomy 31:7–8)
4. 'Now Joshua son of Nun was filled with the spirit of wisdom because Moses had laid his hands on him.' (Deuteronomy 34:9)

If we put these four statements into the likely order of experience, Joshua will be equipped to lead the nation knowing he is:

To be enabled by God's presence

'The LORD himself goes before you and will be with you.' His job will not be to initiate, but to follow and obey the One who will be ahead of him at every turn, in every circumstance and

25

through every difficulty. It is God who will initiate every action in conquering Canaan.

To be empowered by God's Spirit

He is 'a man in whom is the Spirit'. It would be impossible for Joshua to follow God adequately by human resolve alone; only by his dependence upon the Spirit of God – God's agent who makes God's will possible.

To be encouraged by God's people

Moses was to 'encourage and strengthen him'. With the relationship to God being right, Joshua will still need the encouragement, the strength and the fellowship of God's people. He may have to stand out from the crowd from time to time but God's purpose for his people is that they function within the context of the supportive, encouraging, strengthening family of God. No man is called to be an island!

To be equipped by God's wisdom

'Joshua . . . was filled with the spirit of wisdom.' Wisdom is to see things from God's perspective, which is why 'The fear of the LORD is the beginning of wisdom' (Proverbs 9:10). Something greater than human insight and human wisdom will equip him to make the choices necessary as leader of Israel.

All Joshua's previous experience has been preparing him for this day. His commissioning by Moses has reinforced a fundamental truth of Godly leadership: *It is the right man at the right time depending upon the right resources who accomplishes the right ends!* The story of Joshua leading Israel into Canaan does not come out of the blue. God has been preparing, teaching, stretching and equipping his servant for almost forty years after Joshua was first called upon by Moses to lead the army of Israel in their battle with the Amalekites.

ENTERING THE LAND

Joshua 1–4

Joshua 1:1–5

The dawn of a new era – Joshua succeeds Moses

Having led Israel for the forty years since leaving Egypt, Moses has died and a new era has begun. Joshua is appointed by God as Moses' successor, and he is told to prepare himself to lead the Israelites across the Jordan river into Canaan.

 Moses is dead. The leading character of the preceding four books of Scripture has passed from the scene. He did not die of old age, for although he had lived 120 years 'his eyes were not weak nor his strength gone' (Deuteronomy 34:7).

Of the 600,000 fighting men over the age of 20 years when they left Egypt 40 years earlier (Exodus 12:37), as well as the women, only two were about to enter Canaan: Joshua and Caleb. The majority had been sentenced to die in the wilderness 38 years earlier, at Kadesh Barnea, when they had failed to go in and take the land of Canaan which God had offered to them at that time (Numbers 14:30–32). The New Testament states 'they were not able to enter because of their unbelief' (Hebrews 3:19).

Moses' 'unbelief'

It is a sobering thought to realize that Moses was amongst the number of those who died of unbelief. If Moses and Aaron were included in the initial judgment, it was reinforced by their own particular actions later (read Numbers 20:2–13).

However, we must not write Moses off as a failure: he was a man unmatched in his day and throughout Old Testament history. His stature amongst the people of Israel, his concern for the people he served and led, his humble dedication to God, and his personal integrity all set him apart from the rank and file. Yet even this great man died as a consequence of unbelief and disobedience. The lesson of Moses' death is that God is only committed to his own programme and purposes. He is not committed to any person, no matter what his or her history might be, their stature in the eyes of others, or their experience of God in the past.

Joshua's commission

Joshua is God's chosen successor to Moses. The 30-day period of mourning is over (Deuteronomy 34:8). God tells Joshua, 'Now then, you and all these people get ready to cross the Jordan River . . .' (Joshua 1:2). The Jordan river formed the eastern border of Canaan.

The Israelites' victory over the inhabitants of the land was not going to be 'won' so much as to be 'received'. They would be called upon to fight, but to fight battles for which God would take responsibility, and where victory was already assured. Perhaps the greatest quality in men and women of God is the capacity to receive! It is not the capacity to create or to produce that is the mark of spiritual reality and of true Godliness, but the humanity to receive what God alone can give, and to trust what God alone can do.

This raises the question, 'How does God "give" Canaan?' He states, 'I will give you every place where you set your foot' (verse 3). God had already set the land apart for the Israelites and for forty years had been telling them it was theirs to receive. But the enjoyment of God's provision required them to 'set your foot' on the land. This involved deliberate activity on their part. They were to assume the land was theirs and act accordingly, that is, to walk on to it and stake their claim, 'as I promised Moses'.

God's assurance for Joshua

God promised Joshua that, 'No-one will be able to stand up against you all the days of your life. As I was with Moses, so I will be with you' (verse 5). Not only is Joshua here confirmed as Moses' successor, but he is assured that everything God had made available to Moses would be made available to Joshua. Conversely, everything Joshua was to experience in leading Israel in to possess Canaan had been equally available to Moses had he appropriated them and finished the job he had been given to do. Joshua's task was really the unfinished work of Moses and for the task he would have the same resources at his disposal.

Joshua's certainty of success would not derive from any ingenious strategy on his part, nor from his military might, both of which were necessary ingredients in the operation, but which were worthless apart from his dependence upon God himself who promised him, 'I will never leave you nor forsake you' (verse 5). This was the most crucial weapon in his arsenal.

Questions

1. God was to 'give' the land of Canaan to the Israelites. What does God promise to 'give' to the believer today, and how do we appropriate these promises? For example see: Romans 6:23; John 3:34; Romans 15:5; 1 Corinthians 15:57; 2 Corinthians 12:7.

2. If you were Joshua, how would you make the promise of God, 'I will be with you; I will never leave you nor forsake you', a practical reality in the light of the enormous responsibilities and conflicts you were about to face?

3. This section began with the death of Moses. How can we avoid the danger of regarding certain people as indispensable in the work of God rather than trusting God alone? How does this passage help you to face such a situation in your own church or fellowship?

The borders of Israel

Various statements are made in Scripture about the geographical boundaries of Israel. In Joshua 1:4 the area to be occupied by Israel is stated as, 'Your territory will extend from the desert to Lebanon, and from the great river, the Euphrates – all the Hittite country – to the Great Sea on the west'. The area from south to north, 'the desert to Lebanon', presents no problems, and the Mediterranean Sea has always provided the obvious western boundary. But the eastern border of the Euphrates river would give the land a southern border of around 600 miles in distance, more than six times the length ever occupied by Israel. The Euphrates river is mentioned as the eastern border in Genesis 15:18 (there the territory is to stretch from the Nile to the Euphrates); Deuteronomy 1:7; 11:24 and Joshua 1:4. Never in her history has Israel occupied the extent of territory anticipated in these statements.

Perhaps the size of the land, much more than Israel ever occupied, parallels Paul's statement that God, '. . . is able to do immeasurably more than all we ask or imagine, according to his power that is at work within us . . .' (Ephesians 3:20). The boundaries of God's kindness and the extensiveness of his blessing are always so much greater than our experience.

Joshua 1:6-9

Joshua instructed in principles of success

Joshua has been assured by God that he will settle Israel in Canaan, but now turns the attention to Joshua's own responsibilities in the process.

 The land of Canaan is to be given to Israel, and God has stated his responsibility for this outcome. However, God is going to accomplish it through Joshua and gives him some particular instructions. There are two specific things he must do.

- First he is to 'Be strong and very courageous' (verse 6). The fact that God would 'give' the land to the Israelites did not preclude the need for courageous action. The effective activity of God on behalf of his people requires a twin response from them: obedience and trust. Obedience often involves taking risks, but when carried out in the context of an implicit trust in God who gives the orders, the assumption is that God is going to act because he has said he would. Now Joshua is to demonstrate [the same] boldness. Three times God says to Joshua, 'Be strong and [very] courageous' (verses 6, 7, 9), and the people themselves say it to him once (verse 18).

- Secondly he is to 'Be careful to obey all the law my servant Moses gave you' (verse 7). The word 'law' could either be applied to the ten commandments, or to the Pentateuch as a whole (Deuteronomy 31:11). Later it was used also to describe the entire Old Testament (Matthew 5:18) but in this context it clearly refers to the five books of Moses, the entire Scripture Joshua possessed (with the possible addition of the book of Job).

The specific will of God in any situation is always consistent with his overall plan. So God's will for Joshua cannot be outside his plan revealed in 'the law'. Understanding of God's plan is arrived at not by inward meditation but by receiving the word already given, in Joshua's case, by Moses.

Three areas of preoccupation with the law of God are stipulated. It must be

▶ present in the mouth ('Do not let this book . . . depart from your mouth'),

▶ pre-eminent in the mind ('meditate on it day and night'), and

▶ preside over the will ('be careful to do everything written in it').

The law must be present in the mouth

God does not say that the law should not depart from Joshua's ear, but from his mouth! Clearly Joshua was not only to hear and understand the law of God but he was also to declare it. God had told Moses, possibly in reference to Joshua, 'I will raise up for them a prophet like you from among their brothers; I will put my words in his mouth, and he will tell them everything I command him' (Deuteronomy 18:18). Amongst Joshua's other abilities was his effectiveness as a preacher (see Joshua 23). The primary role of spiritual leadership is the clear declaration of what God has said. That priority must never be compromised or belittled. The spiritual leader, preacher or teacher is never called to be original with regard to the content of his message, in fact he must avoid such temptation at all cost. Even Jesus declared, 'My teaching is not my own. It comes from him who sent me' (John 7:16).

The law must be pre-eminent in the mind

Joshua is to 'meditate on it day and night'. To meditate is to concentrate the mind, to think, to contemplate, to explore. It involves the continuous application of the mind to the contemplation of truth. The Bible attributes no special benefits to the memorization of Scripture, but it does, particularly in the Psalms, to the meditation on Scripture (for example Psalms 1:2; 19:14; 77:12; 119:148; 143:5). The result of meditation is familiarity.

The law must preside over the will

The purpose of the revelation from God is '. . . so that you may be careful to do everything written in it'. The law of God is not to enrich our knowledge, but to govern our action. The fuller the obedience, the greater the understanding. There is severe judgment in Scripture on those whose knowledge of the things of God does not lead them to obedience to God (see Matthew 7:21–27; James 4:17; 1 John 2:3–4).

The reason for this strict adherence to the law of God is that '. . . you will be prosperous and successful' (1:8). God has already declared his own purpose to give the land of Canaan to the Israelites, but the experience of his doing so depends upon Joshua's response and co-operation. Once he has fulfilled the obligation God places upon him, prosperity and success are assured to him.

Questions

1. On what grounds does God call Joshua to be 'strong and courageous'? Are there circumstances in which you need to grasp this principle? How will you go about it?
2. Joshua is told to meditate on the law of God, 'day and night'. What are some practical steps you can take to develop the discipline of meditating on the word of God?

3. What are the ingredients of true prosperity and success that God offers to Joshua? How does your conclusion contrast with the expectations of prosperity you find around you?

Joshua 1:10–15

Preparing to enter Canaan

The people are ordered to prepare to cross the Jordan river. The tribes of Reuben, Gad and the half-tribe of Manasseh, already given land east of the Jordan, are reminded of their obligation to fight with their brothers before returning to their own lands.

There is now a series of practical instructions to prepare the people for the crossing of the Jordan river to take possession of the land on the other side. The 'officers of the people' were ordered to get the people ready. These  were representatives of each tribe who had the responsibility of organizing the draft of men into the army, and of making sure there were adequate supplies for the task.

Through the officers, Joshua sent to the Israelites the order, 'Three days from now you will cross the Jordan' (1:11). To mobilize 2 million people was a considerable undertaking and the Israelites would probably need those three days to pack up the camp and prepare to move on. Meanwhile Joshua used those three days of preparation to spy out the land across the Jordan river (see Joshua 2:1–7).

Settlement and responsibility

The last few verses of chapter 1 are addressed specifically to the Reubenites, the Gadites and the half-tribe of Manasseh (verses 12ff). The Reubenites and Gadites were rearers of animals and had already requested of Moses that they make their settlement on the east side of the Jordan, where 'the land was suitable for livestock' (Numbers 32:1), rather than take a share in the land on the west side, currently occupied by the Canaanites. They requested the right to build pens for their livestock and fortified cities for their women and children on the understanding that when the time came to go to war in Canaan their men would arm themselves and fight for the nation, 'until every Israelite has received his inheritance' (Numbers 32:18). Only then would they return to the east side of the Jordan and settle down in their own inheritance. Agreeing to their request, Moses also included the half-tribe of Manasseh in the assigning of this land, although there is no mention of them specifically requesting it. Here Joshua reminds these tribes of this arrangement (verses 12–15) and they carried through their obligation to the end (see 22:1–3 where Joshua commends them for their service before allowing them to return to their wives and children).

The land of rest

The idea of Canaan being described by God as a 'land of rest' is an intriguing and important one. This is not the rest of inactivity. Joshua and the nation were not to be sitting around doing nothing. They were to engage in strenuous activity, but to do so in dependence upon God. There they would experience him to be totally adequate for every situation through which they would go. Joshua, addressing himself to the Reubenites, the Gadites and the half-tribe of Manasseh after the land had been fully conquered, spoke of it as, 'Now that the LORD your God has given your brothers rest as he promised'

(22:4). It was a rest that had involved blood, sweat and tears for Israel, but all the time in dependence upon a power that was not their own – the power of God. 'For anyone who enters God's rest also rests from his own work . . . Let us, therefore, make every effort to enter that rest . . .' (Hebrews 4:10–11). To 'make every effort', and to 'rest from our own work', are not contradictory statements! We must learn to rest in the certainty of God's own sufficiency. This was the invitation of Jesus, 'Come to me, all you who are weary and burdened, and I will give you rest' (Matthew 11:28).

Questions

1. Personal directions given to Joshua have to be adapted to apply to the whole people. Are Joshua's tactics appropriate to the mobilization of the church today?
2. How does corporate responsibility take precedence over personal interests in this section? What principles may we apply from this?
3. How should we understand God's promise of 'rest' in this section? Compare this with Hebrews 4:1–11.

The people affirm loyalty to Joshua

God has made his promises, Joshua has been given his responsibilities and now the people affirm their co-operation by stating the same allegiance to Joshua that they had previously given to Moses.

 The people respond to Joshua's command. It appears as if the response comes only from the two tribes of Reuben and Gad and the half-tribe of Manasseh. However, it seems more likely to have been the response of all the Israelites, which was conveyed to Joshua through the officers of the people (verses 10–11).

Israel's response

They are to do as they are told

'Then they answered Joshua, "Whatever you have commanded us we will do"' (verse 16a). The people must place themselves under the authority of Joshua for he in turn is under the authority of God.

They are to go where they are sent

'. . . and wherever you send us we will go' (verse 16b). They were not to devise strategies of their own but submit themselves to Joshua's direction.

They are to relate to Joshua as they had to Moses

'Just as we fully obeyed Moses so we will obey you' (verse 17). Joshua may not have been too impressed by that promise to him, for the record of the people's obedience to Moses was not particularly impressive! However, the purpose of this statement was to acknowledge and affirm the role of Joshua as God's appointed leader, thereby submitting to him as they had once submitted to Moses. They look for only one qualification: they expect the same affirmation to come from heaven, 'Only may the LORD your God be with you as he was with Moses' (verse 17).

They were to punish those who rebel against Joshua's authority

They state, 'Whoever rebels against your word and does not obey your words . . . will be put to death' (verse 18).

They conclude this affirmation of Joshua with encouragement to him to do what God had earlier commanded, 'Only be strong and courageous'. The implication for the people is that they are willing to join Joshua in running the risks of obedience to God, a risk that the previous generation had conspicuously failed to take during the forty years under Moses' leadership. If Joshua their leader will be strong, they will be strong with him. If he will demonstrate courage, they will join him in courageous action when they face the enemy and take the land. Leadership cannot operate independently of the people. The effective strength of Joshua depends upon the co-operating strength of the people. This had been Moses' downfall at Kadesh Barnea when the people refused to look to God to give them Canaan after the spies returned with their stories of giants stalking the land and of fortified cities with armies they could never conquer.

Questions

1. Having affirmed their obedience to Joshua, the people say, 'Only may the Lord your God be with you'. What does this tell us about the nature of human authority in the church?
2. Rewrite verses 16–18 to address leaders God has placed over you in your church.
3. How are Christians to respect and respond to authority in the world? (Compare Romans 13:1–5.) In what way may we say that secular authority is 'established by God'?

Joshua 2:1–7

Spies in the house of Rahab

Before advancing to Canaan, Joshua sent two spies to investigate the city of Jericho. They were befriended by Rahab, a prostitute, who agreed to hide them in her house.

 Israel were now camped on the east side of the Jordan river, just a little north of the Dead Sea. To enter and occupy Canaan meant that they would need to cross the river and conquer the first city, Jericho, about 7 miles to the west of the Jordan. Joshua sent two spies in advance of the invasion to examine the land in general, though primarily to investigate Jericho.

Thirty-eight years later . . .

The story of the earlier spying and of the land (Numbers 13–14) is discussed on pages 24 and 25.

Now Moses has died, and the people are ready to enter Canaan. God has still promised to give the land to Israel and the subsequent events of crossing the Jordan river, destroying Jericho, and of every victory in battle will be accomplished not by human ingenuity but by divine activity. Their obedience to God will precede and make possible God's activity in response to their trust. Firstly, two spies were sent from the Israelites' base in Shittim to go behind enemy lines in Jericho, 14 miles east of the Israelite camp.

On coming to Jericho the two spies entered the home of the prostitute Rahab. It stands to reason that it was easier for the spies to be inconspicuous in the house of a prostitute. Strangers were her trade and they would be less likely to draw attention to themselves than they would in a more respectable part of the city where unfamiliar visitors were less common. The spies took Rahab into their confidence, declared their business and came to an agreement with her. If she would hide them in her house on the city wall, they would preserve her life and that of her family when they came to conquer the city (verse 14).

Lying pagan commended for her faith

The king of Jericho was told of the presence of these Israelite spies and ordered Rahab to give them up. She fulfilled her part of the bargain to protect them by lying as to their whereabouts. Having hidden them under stalks of flax on the roof of her house she admitted they had come to her earlier in the day but had left at dusk. She didn't know where they had gone, but she urged the messengers to go after them. In the New Testament Rahab is commended for her faith in God (Hebrews 11:31), although not for her lies. It was God who would protect the spies and give the ultimate victory to Israel, and lying would have no part in his strategy.

But Rahab was a pagan prostitute. Denying associations with people and refusing to acknowledge that certain men had been to her home were probably all part of the etiquette of her profession, so she acted normally. Only later was she to meet for herself the God of Israel, and her faith in him, evidenced later in the story, not only results in her being mentioned in the New Testament but brings her into the ancestry of Christ. She married the Israelite Salmon and was the mother of Boaz, the mother-in-law of Ruth and the great-great-grandmother of David (Matthew 1:5).

Questions

1. God promised to give the land to Israel, but this still necessitated action on their part. How does this principle of God promising things yet making demands operate in Christian living today? In this connection, how do you reconcile the statement of 2 Peter 1:3 with the instructions of 2 Peter 1:5-7?
2. Joshua sent spies to explore Jericho in advance of conquering it, even though God had already assured him of victory. Compare this principle with Luke 14:29-33. How would you explain to someone interested in Christ, the cost involved in being a Christian?
3. Rahab is introduced as a prostitute and a liar. On what grounds does the writer to Hebrews commend her for her faith (Hebrews 11:31)?

Joshua 2:8–24

Rahab believes in Israel's victory

Rahab informs the spies that the Canaanites have heard of the Israelites' exploits and their God and are afraid. The spies agree to save Rahab's life if she helps them to escape.

Having effectively diverted the messengers in their search for the spies, Rahab went up on to her roof to speak with the two men before they went to sleep. She told them a remarkable story (verses 9–11).

She mentioned two events in Israel's recent history that had sent waves of fear over the whole country: the opening of the Red Sea (Exodus 14), and the defeat of the two Amorite kings, Sihon and Og (Numbers 21:21–31). The first of these two events had taken place at the outset of Israel's journey some 40 years before and ever since, 'our hearts sank and everyone's courage failed' (verse 11). For nearly 40 years the Israelites had been afraid of the Canaanites (Numbers 13), but for all of that time the Canaanites had actually been afraid of Israel, though to be precise it was Israel's God of whom they were afraid, 'for the LORD your God is God in heaven above and on the earth below' (verse 11). Israel's fear of Canaan derived from their lack of confidence in God. If only they had believed in the power of God as the Canaanites did, then they would have been in Canaan within weeks of leaving Egypt.

Such is Rahab's confidence in God that she speaks of the land being given to Israel already (verse 9). Then she asks for the assurance that her family will be spared death during the destruction of the city. The spies agree to treat all of her relatives kindly, 'when the LORD gives us the land' (verse 14). Rahab, representing the enemy, speaks of victory in the past tense, 'the LORD has given this land to you' (verse 9), but the spies, representing Israel, speak of victory in the future tense, 'when the LORD gives us the land' (verse 14). This is the faith of Rahab that was later commended by the writer to the Hebrews and which enabled her to say, 'The LORD your God is God in heaven above and on the earth below' (verse 11). This has nothing to do with either Israelite or Canaanite tribalism, it has only to do with truth!

Questions

1. Rahab is confident that the Israelites are to be victorious over Jericho. What aspects of the victory won by Jesus Christ do you think are known to the enemy but sometimes doubted by us? List some of the things God has already given you in Christ and ask yourself how much you really believe it.
2. What kind of things do we fear, that are themselves already defeated (for example, see Philippians 4:6–7; 1 Corinthians 15:21–28)?
3. 'Fear' is spoken of several times in this passage. How do you understand the fear of God to be an essential factor in our lives?
4. Rahab's awareness of God was not through hearing his words, but by seeing his works. In what ways ought we to expect the world at large to see the works of God today?

The scarlet cord (verses 15–21)

We must be careful in our use of typology – that is, of making connections between events in the New Testament that are foreshadowed symbolically in the Old Testament – but it is not difficult to see a picture of Christ that has been seen here by many biblical expositors from the early church fathers onwards. The scarlet cord may well have reminded the Israelites of their own salvation in Egypt when the blood of a lamb was placed on the doorpost of their homes, preserving them from the angel of death on that dreadful night when every first-born son in Egypt was put to death. As their salvation had been secured by the scarlet strip of blood, so now, that of Rahab and her family was secured by the scarlet cord. The blood of the passover lamb had been a foretaste of the event when, 'Christ, our passover lamb, has been sacrificed' (1 Corinthians 5:7). There is a scarlet cord running right through the Scriptures that leads to the cross of Christ. He alone can be our protection from the wrath of God, and our only source of salvation.

Joshua 3:1–13

Preparing to cross the Jordan

Joshua led the people from Shittim to the Jordan river. Instructions are given to the Israelites to follow behind the ark of the covenant as they cross the river.

After Joshua heard the encouraging report of the two spies, he led the people from Shittim to the River Jordan, a distance of about 7 miles. Here they set up camp and prepared for the crossing over on to Canaanite territory.

The ark: sign of God's presence

The procedure for crossing the River Jordan was clear. The Levitical priests would carry the ark of the covenant ahead of the people who would move out from their positions and follow behind at a distance of 1,000 yards. The ark was not merely going to show the people the way, it was going to actually make the way. The ark was more than a symbol, like a flag carried in front of an advancing army. It represented the presence of God himself amongst his people (see *The ark of the covenant*, p. 48), and therefore the means of accomplishing what was otherwise impossible. It was God who would bring about the miraculous events necessary to get Israel on to Canaanite territory, and the ark was the physical symbol of his presence. As the priests, carrying the ark, stepped into the Jordan river the water would stop flowing and a path open up through it, enabling them to cross on dry ground (verse 13).

Obedience and trust: signs of Israel's response

God needed consecrated followers. Then he would do amazing things. Once the people had prepared themselves, Joshua told the priests to take up the ark of the covenant and begin the journey. The Lord then made the promise to Joshua, 'Today I will begin to exalt you in the eyes of all Israel, so that they may know that I am with you as I was with Moses' (verse 7). Joshua is linked with Moses nine times in the book of Joshua (see 1:3, 17; 3:7; 4:14, 23–24; 5:15; 8:30–31; 11:15, 23). More is involved, however, than merely the affirmation of Joshua as Moses' successor. Joshua is to enjoy every provision that had been made available for Moses to lead the Israelites into the promised land. Moses had failed to appropriate God's provision then, and had consequently been sentenced to die in the wilderness, along with almost the entire adult generation of Israelites who had left Egypt.

The crossing of the Jordan would be the foretaste of the

ultimate objective, in which God would 'drive out before you the Canaanites, Hittites, Hivites, Perizzites, Girgashites, Amorites and Jebusites' (verse 10), and give the Israelites the land of Canaan. The principle stands true that 'he who began a good work . . . will carry it on to completion' (Philippians 1:6). As the initial crossing into the land would be by divine work, so the occupation of the land would only be by divine power. Dependency upon God at the outset must become the continuous attitude of dependency upon him for everything. The Israelites are reminded that their God is, 'the Lord of all the earth' (verses 11, 13). God's territory and Israel's territory are not the same for the whole earth is God's and it is his privilege to give as he chooses.

Questions

1. What practical lessons can be learned from this story about coping with new situations where 'You have never been this way before' (3:4)?
2. The people are told to 'Consecrate yourselves'. What does this mean? What does it mean for us?
3. God called them for the consecration of Israel, in order that through them he might invade Canaan. In what ways is our consecration going to enable him to invade our world? Are military terms legitimate for us to use of our mission?

The ark of the covenant

The ark of the covenant plays an important role in the early chapters of Joshua. The priests carrying the ark led the way through the Jordan river, and it was carried ahead of the people as they marched around the city of Jericho prior to the collapse of the city walls. Joshua fell face down before the ark after the defeat by Ai when seeking an explanation for the disaster: and the renewal of the covenant at Mount Ebal was carried out as the people stood on either side of the ark. The ark was a rectangular box made of wood and measuring four feet in length, two-and-a-half feet in width and two-and-a-half feet in depth (1.22 m × 76 cm × 76 cm), which was carried on poles inserted into rings, one at each corner. It was covered with gold and its lid was made of pure gold. At each end of the lid was a cherubim made of hammered gold with outstretched wings overshadowing the ark itself (Exodus 25:10–20). The lid was known as the 'mercy seat' (AV) or 'atonement cover' (NIV). The ark originally contained the two tablets of stone upon which had been written the ten commandments, though at some later stage it also contained a gold jar of manna and Aaron's staff that had budded (see Hebrews 9:4). The most important thing about the ark was that God said of it, 'There . . . I will meet with you' (Exodus 25:22). The ark represented the presence of God amongst his people.

When the ark was carried into the River Jordan and later taken around the city walls of Jericho it was a demonstration of the fact that God himself was going to intervene in the situation, so that the people's confidence might be placed in him alone. When many years later the Israelites trusted the ark to deliver them in battle with the Philistines, they were soundly defeated, for it was not the ark that should be trusted but God whom the ark represented (see 1 Samuel 4).

The ark was kept in the inner chamber of the tabernacle, the Most Holy Place (Exodus 26:34 NIV) or Holy of Holies (AV), during the wilderness years, and it was Joshua who set up its more permanent location at Shiloh in the centre of the country (Joshua 18:1).

Joshua 3:14–17

Crossing the Jordan

As the priests stepped in to the River Jordan it dried up, enabling the Israelites to cross on dry ground. The priests carrying the ark remained standing on the river bed until the whole nation had passed by.

It is true that fording the Jordan was possible in a number of places: for example '. . . the road that leads to the fords of Jordan . . .' (Joshua 2:7) and the judge Ehud '. . . taking possession of the fords of the Jordan that led to Moab . . .' (Judges 3:28). In normal circumstances a miracle would not be needed to cross the river. On this occasion however, the Jordan was 'in flood' (verse 15). As the feet of the priests carrying the ark touched the water's edge, the water 'piled up in a heap a great distance away, at a town called Adam in the vicinity of Zarethan, while the water flowing down to the Sea of the Arabah (the Salt Sea) was completely cut off' (verse 16). The distance from Adam to the Salt Sea (the Dead Sea) is more than 20 miles and it would seem the river dried for that entire section. A group of people exceeding 2 million could have marched in a square, 1,000 abreast (approximately a half-mile wide) and 2,000 deep (less than 2 miles in length), and would have required about an hour for them all to pass through the Jordan.

Questions

1. Why do some people find the miraculous events in the Bible difficult to believe? On what basis may we believe them?

2. How did the actions of the Israelites prepare for the miracle of God? What practical lesson can we learn from this?
3. What was the effect of this miracle on the non-Israelites who heard the story (for example, see 4:1)? How do unbelievers react to miracle stories today? What makes a difference?

The miracle of the Jordan

During the entire crossing, the priests who carried the ark of the covenant on their shoulders remained on the dry ground in the middle of the river bed, visibly reiterating the divine nature of this miracle. There have been times in history when the River Jordan has been dammed through natural events. Most recently on 11th July 1927 as the result of an earthquake the river banks caved in and a landslide blocked the river for more than twenty-one hours. A similar event had occurred three years earlier in 1924, and in 1906 the river became so choked with debris following an earthquake that the river bed near Jericho was completely dry for some twenty-four hours. Records of such events go back to December 1267 when some of the high banks of the Jordan collapsed into the river blocking it for ten hours (Werner Keller, *The Bible as History* (rev. edn. Lion and SPCK, 1991, p. 159). Some have therefore suggested that this particular event can be explained in terms of a natural phenomenon, rather than it being a piling up of the water in a way that calls for a supernatural explanation (verse 16). There are several reasons why natural explanations may be discounted.

1. The timing of this crossing was during flood season, when the river was overflowing its banks. To dam the river would have been impossible.

2. The actual break in the water occurred 'as soon as the priests

who carried the ark . . . reached the Jordan and their feet touched the water's edge, the water from upstream stopped flowing' (verses 15–16). Even if there had been a natural cause preventing the flow of the river, the timing itself would have been miraculous.

3. Likewise, exactly as the priests came up out of the water and placed their feet on the river bank 'the waters of the Jordan returned to their place and ran in flood as before' (4:18).

4. The story that circulated amongst the enemy inhabitants of the land was not that of a natural phenomenon, but of supernatural intervention by the Lord over which, 'their hearts sank and they no longer had the courage to face the Israelites' (5:1).

Joshua 4:1–18

Collecting twelve stones

The description of the crossing of the River Jordan by the Israelites is expanded and more details are given. The Israelites collect twelve large stones as a testimony to God's miraculous intervention.

Joshua appointed one man from each of the twelve tribes to take up a stone from the place in the middle of the Jordan where the priests had stood with the ark of the cove-
nant (verse 2). The stones were to be carried to the place where they would set up camp that night, later identified as Gilgal (verse 19). They were to be of reasonable size: 'Each of you is to take up a stone on his shoulder . . .' (verse 5), and their objective

was to set up a monument as a sign to succeeding generations of the deliverance they had experienced at God's hand. This was not an impromptu idea of Joshua's for in chapter 3:12, in advance of crossing the Jordan, he had instructed the people to choose one man from each tribe, though the reason for this was not made clear at the time. It was after the whole nation had finished crossing the Jordan safely that these twelve men were sent back for the stones (verse 1).

Stories with a meaning

It would seem that two stone memorials were built by the twelve men who had gathered the stones. One was built on the river bed at the precise point where the priests carrying the ark had stood (verse 9), and the other in Gilgal where they made camp (verse 19). The one in Gilgal reminded the people of *what* had happened, the memorial on the river bed showed the people *where* it had happened, of which the writer states, 'And they are there to this day' (verse 9), presumably visible when the Jordan ran low.

In both cases the memorial stones would provoke the children to question (verses 6, 21). The use of symbols to provoke questions and to teach God's people is seen in other parts of Scripture. The expression, 'When your children ask you, "What do these stones mean?"', is reminiscent of Exodus 12:26–27 and Deuteronomy 6:20–25. In Exodus 12, after giving details of the passover meal of unleavened bread that would precede the tenth and final plague on Egypt and Israel's consequent release from captivity, Moses instructed the people to observe the ceremony annually when they entered Canaan. 'And when your children ask you, "What does this ceremony mean to you?", then tell them, "It is the Passover sacrifice to the LORD, who passed over the houses of the Israelites in Egypt and spared our homes when he struck down the Egyptians"' (Exodus 12:26–27). This was a memorial to God bringing Israel out of Egypt, and its celebration was designed to remind the people of God's miraculous intervention on their behalf. The passover was a memorial celebration of their coming *out* of Egypt, the stones of Gilgal a memorial to their coming *in* to Canaan.

Laws with a purpose

In Deuteronomy 6 a similar statement is made after restating the ten commandments. 'In the future, when your son asks you, "What is the meaning of the stipulations, decrees and laws the LORD God has commanded you?" tell him: "We were slaves of Pharaoh in Egypt, but the LORD brought us out of Egypt with a mighty hand . . . But he brought us out from there to bring us in and give us the land that he promised on oath to our forefathers"' (Deuteronomy 6:20–21, 23). The law would provoke the children to question their parents, in answer to which the parents would point the children to the purpose of God in bringing them out of Egypt to enjoy his full provision in Canaan. In the context of their deliverance *from* Egypt and in *to* Canaan, the law revealed the way in which God demanded they should live their lives.

Promises fulfilled

The role of the men of Reuben, Gad and the half-tribe of Manasseh (verses 12–13) is mentioned because these tribes had already been allotted land on the east of the Jordan, but had agreed with Moses to leave their territory to join the other tribes in conquering the land of Canaan (see Numbers 32, Joshua 1:12–18). Of these tribes 40,000 men armed for war crossed the Jordan (verse 12).

In the census of the Israelite tribes taken by Moses, which lists men over the age of 20 years able to serve in the Israelite army, the tribe of Reuben numbered 43,730 eligible men (Numbers 26:7); Gad numbered 40,500 (Numbers 26:18) and the half-tribe of Manasseh numbered 52,700 (Numbers 26:34), a total of 146,930. Approximately one-third of this total crossed over the Jordan with the rest of Israel. The majority therefore remained east of the Jordan, no doubt to protect and provide for the women and children, and their herds.

As a result of the crossing of the Jordan, Joshua is confirmed before the people as the successor to Moses and 'they revered him all the days of his life' (verse 14). They had already promised to obey Joshua as they had obeyed Moses (1:17); now they revered him in the same way too.

Questions

1. What events in our lives may have provoked the question, 'What does this mean?' (see 4:6–7) enabling us to bear witness to Christ?
2. 'That day the Lord exalted Joshua in the sight of all Israel' (4:14). How did God do that, and why do you think it was important (cf. 3:7). How do we recognize the call of God to our leaders?
3. How can physical symbols be used to reveal aspects of the gospel to the world? Give some specific examples.

Joshua 4:19–24

The Red Sea and the Jordan

A comparison between Joshua crossing the River Jordan and Moses crossing the Red Sea.

Israel set foot in Canaan on the 'tenth day of the first month' (1:19). This was a significant date, for it was on the tenth day of the first month that the passover was first enacted and later celebrated (Exodus 12:2–3) exactly 40 years before. The following verses (4:21–24) compare the way Israel had been brought *out* of Egypt, with the way they had been brought *in* to Canaan. We have already commented on the memorial stones set up at Gilgal, and the passover celebration that would both provoke the curiosity of the children, 'When your children ask you . . .' (see comments on 4:1–18). Another similarity is highlighted: 'The LORD your God did to the Jordan just what he had done to the Red Sea when he dried it up before us until we had passed over' (verse 23). God had performed a similar miracle to bring Israel *in* to Canaan as he had done to bring them *out* of Egypt. All of this, explained Joshua, is to let you know that as it took God to bring you *out* of your bondage and slavery, so it takes God to bring you *in* to the land of provision and plenty. From beginning to end the whole activity is possible only in dependency upon God.

Our spiritual experience

This is an obvious and clear picture of spiritual experience. In the New Testament the passover is a picture of Christ, 'the Lamb of God who takes away the sin of the world' (John 1:29). Canaan is depicted as the position of rest in the full sufficiency of Christ where we may 'rest from our own work' and find all the resources we need in him (Hebrews 4). The means by which we come out of sin (Egypt) is identical to the means by which we enter the fullness of Christ (Canaan). In both cases God was the author, the provider and the sustainer. Paul wrote, 'So then, just as you received Christ Jesus as Lord, continue to live in him . . .' (Colossians 2:6). The way we *receive* him in repentance and faith, turning from what we are and allowing him to do for us what only he can do, is also the way we are *to live*, in repentance and faith, turning from what we are and allowing him to do what only he can do! For 40 years the Israelites had wandered in the wilderness precisely because they did not allow God to take them *in* as he had once brought them *out*! (Numbers 13–14).

Acts and attitudes

Although the celebration of the passover and the twelve stones piled up at Gilgal were tributes to God's working, there was an important difference in the memorials by which both occasions were to be remembered. The celebration of their coming out was to take place only once a year. It took place on the tenth day of the first month, the exact date of their departure from Egypt. But the memorial to their entering Canaan, the twelve stones at Gilgal, was placed as a permanent reminder, visible and to be appropriated every day of the year. Coming out of Egypt was a historical event, never again to be repeated in their experience.

The occupation of Canaan, to fulfil the purpose for which God had placed them there, was a daily act of worship to God that acknowledged that only in his strength and power they would fulfil his purposes. As an *act* of faith in Christ once brought us out of our sin, it is an *attitude* of faith in Christ that enables us every day to live a life of usefulness and purpose. 'He did this so that all the peoples of the earth might know that the hand of the LORD is powerful and so that you might always fear the LORD your God' (4:24). The crisis event of the moment must lead to a process of living that continues every day.

Questions

1. Sometimes God instructs the creating of memorials to his work (for example, 4:20–24). Share some personal 'memorials' you may have which testify to God working in your life (for example places, events, experiences).
2. What place, if any, do you think memorials to acts of God should have in the church? How important is the Lord's Supper/Holy Communion?
3. What significance do you see in the comparison between God

opening the Red Sea as the Israelites came out of Egypt, and his opening of the Jordan river as they came into Canaan (see 4:23–24)?

CONQUERING THE LAND

Joshua 5–12

Circumcision at Gilgal

The Israelites set foot on Canaanite territory for the first time, striking fear in the hearts of its inhabitants. They renew the ritual of circumcision which had been neglected.

 The immediate result of the miraculous crossing of Jordan was the intimidation of the Canaanite kings. They were totally deflated, 'their hearts sank and they no longer had the courage to face the Israelites' (verse 1). It was not that the Israelites impressed them, but that they had heard how, 'the LORD dried up the Jordan before the Israelites' (verse 1). It was not fear of Israel, but fear of God! People will not be challenged by anything we might do for God: it is only as we realize our inherent weakness and allow God to do things for us that people will take notice!

It was at that time that God gave Joshua the order to 'circumcise the Israelites again' (verse 2). This was not a repeat operation on any of the men, but the re-establishing of a ritual neglected during the 40 years in the wilderness.

The reason why baby boys were not circumcised in the 40-year wandering would seem to be sheer neglect. Although God had so dramatically confronted Moses with the need to circumcise his own children, there is no evidence that Moses ever took this seriously enough to encourage, much less to insist, that the people he led observe the ritual, although he was told by God that no-one could celebrate the passover before being circumcised (see Exodus 12:44, 48). There are two references in the wilderness years to circumcising the heart (Deuteronomy 10:16; 30:6) but not to circumcising the body. On the other hand, perhaps the judgment of God at Kadesh Barnea when he promised that the adult population who had left Egypt would never enter Canaan (Numbers 13–14) removed from them a sense of purpose in circumcision which, as we have already shown, was bound up with the promise of occupying the land – a promise they now knew they would not live long enough to experience.

After the whole nation had been circumcised, the people remained in the camp for three days until they were healed. They named the place Gibeath Haaraloth (verse 3), meaning 'hill of foreskins', though it has become better known as Gilgal which may mean 'rolling', identifying the Lord's statement, 'Today I have rolled away the reproach of Egypt from you' (verse 9).

Questions

1. The Amorite kings' 'hearts sank' when they heard how God had dried up the Jordan. What is the demonstration of God's power that lies at the heart of the gospel, and why is it relevant to those outside of Christ? (See 1 Corinthians 15, especially verses 25–26.)
2. The rite of circumcision and the celebration of the passover are outward signs of the covenant between God and Israel. What New Testament equivalents are there to this, and what are their benefits to us personally as well as to the church corporately?

3. In what ways are outward signs of a relationship with God a help to our witness in the world? In what ways may they be a hindrance?

Circumcision

Circumcision was commanded by God to Abraham as 'the sign of the covenant between me and you' (Genesis 17:9–14). God's covenant with Abraham and his descendants was thereby acknowledged and the terms of it agreed to in this surgical act carried out on eight-day-old boys. The rite was performed throughout the Egyptian period of the Israelites' history, though during the years in the wilderness it was neglected. Hence the command of God to Joshua at Gilgal that he must circumcise all the males who had been born since they left Egypt, that is, all under the age of forty, as part of the process of renewing the covenant. In Abraham's case, circumcision followed his personal act of trust in God and was a sign of his faith (Romans 4:10–12), though thereafter the sign was of a covenant already established between Israel and God, and which, by virtue of birth into Israel the young Israelite was already a participant (Amos 3:2). Being the chosen people was not an option, hence they stood answerable to God on the grounds of this special relationship. In later years, the physical act tended to be seen as all-important, to the neglect of the spiritual reality to which it was a testimony ('Circumcise yourselves to the LORD, circumcise your hearts . . .' Jeremiah 4:4). The role of circumcision brought the first major debate to the early church (Acts 15:1ff), where it was decreed to be not only irrelevant to the new covenant but that to insist upon it was to rob the people of the sufficiency of Christ alone, and therefore to be an enemy of the gospel (Galatians 5:2–6).

Joshua 5:10–12

The passover and the end of manna

The Israelites re-established the passover celebration for the first time in 39 years. The next day the manna that had been faithfully and miraculously provided by God for 40 years ceased, and instead the people enjoyed the rich produce of the land.

On the fourteenth day of the month, four days after crossing the Jordan and three days after the mass circumcision of all males under 40 years, the Israelites celebrated the pass-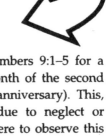over for the first time in 39 years (see Numbers 9:1–5 for a record of it being celebrated in the first month of the second year after leaving Egypt, that is, the first anniversary). This, unlike circumcision, may not have been due to neglect or disobedience, for the original instructions were to observe this ceremony, 'when you enter the land' (Exodus 12:25). However, after the events at Kadesh Barnea during the second year, the people would have little reason to celebrate in any case, for they had been doomed to die in the desert on account of their disobedience. Most were sorry they had ever left Egypt and all knew they had no prospect of enjoying Canaan, so what was there to celebrate? But now the chosen people of God were on Canaanite territory for the first time since the eleven sons of Israel had left to join their brother Joseph in Egypt, more than four centuries before. The passover was now to become one of the major annual feasts in Canaan.

The shadow and the real thing

The Israelites could have travelled the less than 300 miles distance from Egypt to Canaan in a few weeks at most (cf. Deuteronomy 1:2). Instead, because of their disobedience and unbelief it took 40 years. And yet it did not lead God to abandon them in the desert but to sustain them albeit with a substance that would never satisfy them and which was only an imitation of the real thing. God did not satisfy them in the desert with the daily supply of manna for his intention was to satisfy them only in Canaan, where they would feast on the real thing.

God had intended Israel to travel immediately to Canaan where they would enter and occupy the land. They did not do so, and to sustain them in the desert they were fed with something (manna, see Exodus 16:31) that looked and tasted like the real thing, but which was not the real thing and could not satisfy them as only the real thing would (the milk and honey of the promised land). It became a consistent source of frustration and grumbling amongst the people. The whole scenario may be taken as a picture of being sealed with the Holy Spirit (Ephesians 1:13–14), yet not being filled with the Holy Spirit (Ephesians 5:18). It is the difference between being sustained by the Spirit, but not satisfied by the Spirit.

Forty years after manna was first provided to sustain Israel, they crossed into Canaan and the people began to feast on the rich provision of the land for the very first time and 'the manna stopped the day after they ate this food from the land' (verse 12). This was no coincidence, for God will only satisfy his people in the right place. The only way to be satisfied with God is to give all of one's life to him, to rest in the Canaan of the fullness of Christ (Hebrews 4). Anything less than that may sustain us, for we have been eternally saved, but it will not satisfy us. This is the primary message of the provision of manna, which ceased when Israel celebrated the passover in the land God had provided for them.

Questions

1. The manna was a foreshadowing of Christ (John 6:31–35). Name or list some of the aspects of his person and ministry that come to mind in this respect.
2. What is the significance of the manna stopping the day after the Israelites ate the food of Canaan? Has this any meaning for us?
3. What do you think are some of the basic needs for which the world at large is hungry, and that are available to them in Christ?

Joshua 5:13–15

The commander of the army of the LORD

Joshua meets the 'commander of the army of the LORD'. The commander's words to Joshua are prefaced with the significant instruction to take off his shoes, a similar command to that given to Moses at the burning bush.

As Joshua approached Jericho, he confronted a stranger (verse 13). This must have been one of several pre-incarnate appearances of Christ, particularly as he is later described as 'the LORD' (6:2) (see *Theophany*). As 'commander of the army of the LORD' he has not come to take sides but to take over.

Joshua's response was to 'fall face down to the ground in reverence', thereby acknowledging the stranger's superior status, and to ask, 'What message does my Lord have for his servant?' (verse 13). If there is any uncertainty as to the status of this man, his instruction, 'Take off your sandals, for the place where you are standing is holy' (verse 15), removes all doubt. This is reminiscent of God's instructions to Moses at the burning bush (Exodus 3:5). It is another of the parallels between Moses and Joshua.

An exchange of shoes!

Why did God instruct Joshua to take off his shoes? Why had he instructed Moses earlier to do the same? Was it just a cultural point, a mark of respect or reverence? There may be a deeper reason. Later the Lord states, 'I have delivered Jericho into your hands' (6:2). It was the commander of the army of the LORD who would conquer Jericho, but he would not do it independently of Joshua and the people, he would do it through them. He would do it in Joshua's shoes! He had earlier asked Moses to take off his shoes for a similar reason. Although it was God who would bring Israel out of Egypt, Moses would be his instrument in the process. It would be God in Moses' shoes. Now, as with Moses earlier, he asks Joshua for the surrender of his shoes for although it is God who will take Jericho and give them Canaan, Joshua will be his instrument – God will do it in Joshua's shoes.

The surrender of our feet is important to God. Isaiah wrote, 'How beautiful on the mountains are the feet of him who brings good news' (Isaiah 52:7; Nahum 1:15). Why did he not say, 'How beautiful is the mouth, or the lips, or the personality, or the mind, or the voice of him who brings good news'? Why does he specify 'the feet'? I suggest the first part of our anatomy God needs if he is going to do his work through us is our feet. He needs to place our feet in the right place before our hands or lips can fulfil the right task.

Feet first

God had told Moses, 'Every place where you set your foot will be yours' (Deuteronomy 11:24). There was nothing particularly special about Moses' feet except that God was in his shoes, and therefore his feet now carried authority. Part of God's purpose in creating man is stated as, 'You put everything under his feet' (Psalm 8:6). Once Moses had taken off his shoes and his feet were placed on holy ground they in turn would occupy territory. In a similar way God had said to Joshua, 'I will give you every place where you set your foot' (Joshua 1:3). Joshua had now arrived in the land where he encountered a physical manifestation of God, and his shoes are the first thing the commander of the army of the Lord required of him. From now on the placing of his feet is going to be the means of occupying territory.

Questions

1. What does the appearance of the Lord as 'a man with a drawn sword in his hand' (Joshua 5:13) tell you about the character of God?
2. If God requires the surrender of our feet what other parts of the body does Scripture speak specifically about making available to God? Find verses for each (e.g., ears, eyes, mouth etc.).
3. What does the revelation of God as the 'commander of the army of the LORD' tell you about God's involvement in the worldwide mission of the church?

Theophany/Christophany

The appearance of the man standing with a drawn sword in his hand as Joshua was about to take Jericho, should be understood as a theophany (or Christophany) that is, a physical manifestation of God. There are a number of instances of God appearing in some material form, primarily as 'the angel of the LORD' or as a man. Below are some examples.

As the angel of the LORD

The expression occurs over fifty times in the Old Testament: to Hagar (Genesis 16:7–13; 21:17); to Abraham (Genesis 22:11–18); to Jacob (Genesis 31:11); to Moses (Exodus 3:2); to Gideon (Judges 6:11–24); to Manoah's wife (Judges 13:3–25).

As a human being

To Abraham (Genesis 18:1–33); to Jacob (Genesis 32:24–32); to Joshua (Joshua 5:13–15).

The physical voice of God

In the Garden of Eden (Genesis 3:8); a 'still small voice' to Elijah (1 Kings 19:11–18); the voice from heaven at the baptism of Jesus (Matthew 3:17); at his transfiguration (Matthew 17:5); and during his time in Jerusalem before his arrest (John 12:28).

Other material manifestations of God

As flame in the burning bush (Exodus 3:2–6); as smoke, fire and thunder on Mount Sinai (Exodus 19:18–20).

The physical appearance of God comes to its climax in the person of Christ, though this should be seen as altogether different to the manifestations in the Old Testament. After the ascension of Christ, he appeared in physical form both to Paul (Acts 9:17; 22:14; 1 Corinthians 15:8), and to John (Revelation 1:12ff).

Joshua 6:1–5

Preparing to conquer Jericho

Now that Israel is in Canaan the first city to be conquered is Jericho, a city already in fear of Israel on account of God's dealings with them. God assures Joshua that Jericho is ready to be given into their hands.

Jericho is described as being 'tightly shut up' (verse 1). Clearly the fear of the kings throughout Canaan after the miraculous crossing of the Jordan river (5:1) applied to the inhabitants of Jericho. Rahab had told the two spies that fear had overcome the people on hearing how God had acted on their behalf (2:8–11). Now the gates to the city were barred: 'No-one went out and no-one came in' (verse 1), and presumably their armed men and weapons were in position to defend the city. From outside the city appears impenetrable.

Mission impossible

However, this impossible situation only underlines the statement of the Lord to Joshua: 'I have delivered Jericho into your hands along with its king and its fighting men' (6:2). For a nomadic tribe, who have spent 40 years living in tents in the desert, there could be no hope of victory over an experienced strongly fortified city like Jericho under their own natural resources. Gaining victory was not to be the business of the people. Their task was obedience to 'the commander of the army of the LORD' (5:14), and ensuring victory would be his business.

This was not a new promise for God had several times

declared, 'You are now about to cross the Jordan to go in and dispossess nations greater and stronger than you, with large cities that have walls up to the sky . . . But be assured today that the LORD your God is the one who goes across ahead of you like a devouring fire. He will destroy them; he will subdue them before you' (Deuteronomy 9:1, 3). The promise of God's victory did not render the people motionless however. God's victory is only demonstrated in the context of obedience to his instructions, whilst at the same time trusting in his power.

There are a number of significant points in this story.

▶ The frequency of the number seven. Seven priests were to carry seven trumpets; the march around the city was to take place every day for seven days, the final day marching seven times around. We must be cautious of rigid views of numerology, but there is no doubt that seven in Scripture signifies completion and is associated with the activity of God rather than the activity of man.

▶ The carrying of the ark of the covenant, as in the crossing of the Jordan, signifies the presence of God as crucial to the operation.

▶ The loud shout at the end of the seventh encircling of the city on the seventh day would precipitate the fall of the city walls, but pointedly without the Israelites lifting a finger to touch, or push, or attack. All these factors proclaim one thing: the defeat of Jericho was the work of God, not the Israelites.

Archaeological evidence seems to have produced conflicting theories at different times about the city of Jericho and its walls at the time of this conquest. There is evidence of the walls having to be rebuilt seventeen times over the 1500-year period of the early and middle Bronze Age (Werner Keller, *The Bible as History* (rev. edn. Lion and SPCK, 1991), p. 162). It is therefore difficult to pinpoint the exact size of the city at this time, or precise details about the walls. The message of this chapter is that victory over Jericho was won by God and received by the people.

Questions

---

1. Who is in charge of your life's battles? Who gives the orders and who obeys? Discuss what it means to live under authority.
2. God gave no reasons for Israel needing to march around Jericho over seven days. Are you conscious of commands God has given you but do not understand the reasons? What should be your attitude in such situations?
3. God did not grant Israel immediate victory over Jericho without the process of disciplined obedience and patience. What can we learn from this about reaching people for Christ?

Joshua 6:6–27

Seven days around the city

God's instructions to Israel were very specific. A recurring principle in Joshua is that action on God's part is in response to the people's obedience. This principle holds true here.

The instructions for conquering Jericho were given by the stranger who appeared with the drawn sword, 'the commander of the army of the LORD,' later identified as the Lord himself. He is not mentioned again and presumably, insofar as his physical presence was concerned, left the scene. What he commanded is now carried out. Joshua obeyed in detail the instructions he had been given. On the seventh march around the city on the seventh day, Joshua commanded the people, 'Shout! For the LORD has given you the city' (verse 16).

To shout was affirmation of their confidence that God was going to work on their behalf, but having destroyed the walls the people were to march in and mop up the city. Joshua reminded the people that only Rahab and her household were to be saved, in accordance with the agreement she made with the two spies (2:12–14). He gave them instructions that all the silver, gold and articles of bronze and iron were declared sacred to the Lord and must go into his treasury (verse 19). To tamper with these and take any for themselves would bring destruction and trouble (verse 18). This severe warning is in keeping with the Mosaic law, '. . . nothing a man owns and devotes to the LORD . . . may be sold or redeemed . . . No person devoted to destruction may be ransomed: he must be put to death' (Leviticus 27:28–29).

Now the actual conquering of the city takes place. The people shout, the walls collapse and the armed men charge straight in and take the city. They put to death people and livestock alike, preserving only Rahab's family who had taken refuge in her house. They were taken to a safe place outside the city, whilst the city itself was torched and burned to the ground. Before the final destruction they took the silver, gold and articles of bronze and iron into the treasury of the Lord's house, as they had been instructed.

Rahab blessed, Jericho cursed

Rahab is spoken of as being spared in verses 22–23 and again in verse 25, along with all who belonged to her, and is declared as 'living among the Israelites to this day' (verse 25). She is never mentioned again in the book of Joshua, but her role was to be significant. She married a man named Salmon and they had a son Boaz. He married Ruth, the widowed Moabitess, who had returned to Israel with her mother-in-law after both of their husbands had died and who in turn became the grandmother of Jesse, the father of David. Rahab therefore was the great-great-grandmother of David, and an ancestor of Christ (Matthew 1:5–6).

On destroying the city, Joshua pronounced a curse stating that anyone who undertakes to rebuild it will do so at the cost of his first-born son and setting up its gates will be at the expense of his youngest son. The permanent destruction of a city that had turned away from God and worshipped other gods was laid down earlier (Deuteronomy 13:16). Blessing and cursing were part of the structures of discipline set up by God in the covenant with Moses (Deuteronomy 27). Joshua's curse on Jericho was fulfilled more than four centuries later in the time of King Ahab when, 'Hiel of Bethel rebuilt Jericho. He laid its foundation at the cost of his firstborn son Abiram and he set up its gates at the cost of his youngest son Segub, in accordance with the word of the LORD spoken by Joshua son of Nun' (1 Kings 16:34).

Chapter 6 concludes with the confirmation of God's presence with Joshua. 'So the LORD was with Joshua, and his fame spread throughout the land' (verse 27). Two things are stressed: the presence and activity of God with Joshua, which is the recurring emphasis of the book (see 1:5; 2:10; 3:7; 4:14; 5:1 etc.), and the exaltation of Joshua as the leader of Israel, which God had declared he would bring about (3:7).

Questions

1. God brought down the walls of Jericho as Israel obeyed everything he told them. Think of some promises of God that are conditional upon obedience to his command.
2. Discuss the relationship between divine activity, 'The LORD has given you the city' (Joshua 6:16), and the human responsibility of going in to fight.
3. What parallels do you think can be seen between the salvation of Rahab's household and New Testament salvation?

The killing of seemingly innocent people

A disturbing feature of the book of Joshua is the mass slaughter of seemingly innocent people. On conquering Jericho the Israelite army '. . . destroyed with the sword every living thing in it – men and women, young and old, cattle, sheep and donkeys' (6:21), preserving only the family of Rahab. God had stated before Israel entered Canaan that '. . . in the cities of the nations the LORD your God is giving you as an inheritance, do not leave alive anything that breathes. Completely destroy them – the Hittites, Amorites, Canaanites, Perizzites, Hivites and Jebusites – as the LORD your God has commanded you' (Deuteronomy 20:16–17). That is a comprehensive order to annihilate everyone and everything.

Barbaric as that may seem, a reason is given for this: 'Otherwise, they will teach you to follow all the detestable things they do in worshipping their gods, and you will sin against the LORD your God' (Deuteronomy 20:18). This is the key to understanding this action. The people were not innocent as we might suppose, but guilty of detestable practices that had provoked the wrath of God over a sufficiently long period so that his judgment on them was just. God anticipated the depth of depravity to which the inhabitants of Canaan would sink when he said to Abraham, 'In the fourth generation your descendants will come back here, for the sin of the Amorites has not yet reached its full measure' (Genesis 15:16). At the time of Israel's defeat of the northern kings it is stated that, '. . . it was the LORD himself who hardened their hearts to wage war against Israel, so that he might destroy them totally, exterminating them without mercy, as the LORD had commanded Moses' (Joshua 11:20). To some this places the onus of responsibility upon God who, it is stated, hardened their hearts. But this would be a mistaken understanding. The activity of God had the effect of solidifying the disposition of the people towards God. In such a case, to have brought about a hardening of the people's hearts in this way is not to be responsible for their disposition in the first place which led to this result (see 11:16–23).

In every expression of God's wrath we are to trust the question Abraham put in a similar circumstance: 'Will not the judge of all the earth do right?' (Genesis 18:25). See also the ways that Jesus treated people, especially women and children, as portrayed in the gospels.

Joshua 7:1–9

The sin of Achan

Victory over Jericho is followed by defeat in the battle against Ai as a result of Achan's sin, and God's presence is withdrawn from Israel.

After their victory over Jericho, Israel moved on to the next city, Ai, and were defeated. Their defeat was not due to the military superiority of Ai, though perhaps Israel was  over-confident of victory after their overwhelming defeat of Jericho. Two spies sent to Ai reported back: 'Send two or three thousand men to take it and do not weary all the people' (verse 3). The reason for their defeat was not overconfidence, however, the reason was sin.

Israel guilty

The first verse sets the scene for what is to follow. Achan, introduced as the son of Carmi, grandson of Zimri, great-grandson of Zerah and of the tribe of Judah, took some of the 'devoted things', the silver, gold, bronze and iron that were declared sacred to the Lord (6:19), during the destruction of Jericho, so that 'the LORD's anger burned against Israel' (verse 1). In effect Achan stole from God, for to deny God what is his is to steal from him (Malachi 3:8–10). Achan alone does not stand responsible. Although only Achan's name is mentioned, his sin is attributed to the whole nation and all suffer the consequences. God declared, 'Israel has sinned; they have violated my covenant . . . They have taken some of the devoted things; they have stolen, they have lied, they have put them with their own possessions' (verse 11). Here a principle holds true: 'the result of one trespass was condemnation for all men' (Romans 5:18). Ultimately Achan stood responsible for his sin, but God dealt with his people corporately. Sin in one contaminated the whole.

Israel careless

Unaware of the tragedy that would befall them because of Achan's sin Joshua sent men to attack Ai, assuming an easy victory. The exact location of Ai is difficult to pinpoint. It is described in the text as 'near Beth Aven to the east of Bethel' (verse 2). The names of these two towns, from which Ai is given its bearing, are in complete contrast to each other. Beth Aven means 'house of iniquity' in contrast to Bethel which means 'house of God'. Beth Aven remained true to its name, for centuries later it was still referred to as a place for worship of a calf-idol (Hosea 10:5). At least we know from this location that Ai was somewhere up in the Judean hills, north of Jerusalem, and was inhabited by Amorites (verse 7), one of the peoples occupying Canaan.

Joshua had sent two spies to reconnoitre the area who, on their return, reported that two or three thousand men would be sufficient to take Ai for 'only a few men are there' (verse 3). The total population of Ai was in fact 12,000 (8:25). Against that number two or three thousand fighting men might be a realistic figure, though perhaps a little low, to be confident of victory in normal circumstances. Another reason for proposing that only a small number should fight against Ai was so as not to 'weary all the people' (verse 3). All the upheaval of moving across the Jordan and taking Jericho was having its toll. Joshua opted for the higher of these estimates and dispatched 3,000 men.

Israel devastated

The journey to Ai was uphill, a climb of more than 1,000 metres. The battle was a disaster for Israel: the people of Ai killed 36 Israelites, and pursued the rest to some stone quarries. The impact on the people was devastating: 'At this the hearts of the people melted and became like water' (verse 5). Interestingly, this description of Israel's fear is very similar to the description of the Amorites' fear earlier (5:1), and also Rahab's description of the Canaanites' fear (2:9). When Joshua heard the news he 'tore his clothes and fell face down to the ground before the ark of the LORD' (verse 6). The elders of Israel joined him in displaying the customary expressions of grief, tearing their clothes and putting dust on their heads. Joshua's first response is to assume God has failed them (verses 7–9). There is no indication that he considered the fault to be theirs, or engaged in any immediate examination of his own people. He even suggests to God that it was a mistake to have ever come across the Jordan in the first place (verse 7), a cry reminiscent of the Israelites in the desert who wished they had never left Egypt (Numbers 14:2–4). It was not just the loss of this battle that troubled Joshua, but the Israelites' loss of morale and loss of face before their enemies, who as a consequence regained their morale: 'they will hear about this . . . surround us and wipe out our name from the earth' (verse 9).

Questions

1. Joshua's first assumption when defeated by Ai was to assume that God had failed them. In what circumstances do we, or others, tend to blame God for things that go wrong? How should we answer the common assumption that God could have prevented trouble? In this case the experience of failure had sin as its cause. Is this always so?
2. What can we learn from the statement, 'The Israelites acted unfaithfully', when we know it was one man who was guilty of wrongdoing?
3. What areas of obvious failure in the church do you think weaken our effectiveness in the world? What should we do about this? What are the biblical reasons for your conclusions?

Joshua 7:10–26

The sentence of God

God explains to Joshua why the Israelites were defeated at Ai: they have sinned against him. Achan is identified and punished by death.

God was there but where were you?

Joshua has complained before the Lord and God's reply comes as a rebuke to him: 'Stand up! What are you doing down on your face?' (verse 10). There is a time to be on bended knees before God but this was not it. Joshua was looking in the wrong place for an explanation of the disaster. It was not the faithfulness of God that was in question but the faithlessness of the people: 'Israel has sinned' (verse 11). God does not at this point identify the culprit, but addresses the greater issue of the breaking of the agreement which bound them corporately to him, and he to them: 'they have been made liable to destruction. I will not be with you any more . . .' (verse 12). This statement, 'I will not be with you any more', refers to his active presence amongst them. It could read, 'I will not work on your behalf any more'. This principle is clearly set out in a statement made by the prophet Azariah to Asa, king of Judah, many years later: 'The LORD is with you when you are with him' (2 Chronicles 15:2). We need not ask God to 'be with us'; rather, it is our business to 'be with him'. Joshua's prayer to God says in effect, 'Where were you?' God's reply is 'Where were you?' God had not failed. The people had failed: 'they have violated my covenant . . . they have taken . . . stolen . . . lied' (verse 11). Unless and until this is addressed and dealt with they will live forever in defeat: 'You cannot stand against your enemies until you remove it' (verse 13).

Detection

The procedure for discovering those responsible for the crime was set out by God. The Lord would first identify the responsible tribe; from the tribe he would identify the responsible clan; from the clan he would identify the responsible family; from the family he would identify the responsible individual, and the man was Achan.

Joshua called on Achan to confess his crime: 'My son, give glory to God . . . Tell me what you have done; do not hide it from me' (verse 19). Achan gave a full confession.

Sentence

The sentence that followed was severe: 'Then Joshua together with all Israel, took Achan . . . the silver, the robe, the gold wedge, his sons and daughters, his cattle, donkeys and sheep, his tent and all that he had to the Valley of Achor' (verse 24). There all Israel joined in stoning him, followed by the rest of his family and livestock, finally burning their remains. All Israel had come under judgment as a result of this sin, so all Israel shared in carrying out the punishment. The measure of the punishment suffered by Achan and his family is in keeping with the Mosaic law (see Deuteronomy 13:12-18). The law forbade the punishment of children for their fathers' sins and vice versa (Deuteronomy 24:12), so, although this passage doesn't record the part Achan's family played in the theft, it is safe to assume that they were also involved. They shared in Achan's punishment and the whole family and their entire possessions were destroyed.

Hope

Having stoned and burned Achan and his family, 'the LORD turned from his fierce anger' (verse 26); and the people heaped a large pile of rocks over the remains and called that place the Valley of Achor which means 'trouble'. That name continued throughout Israel's history and the one redeeming feature of the whole episode is that God could say to Hosea, 'I will . . . make the Valley of Achor a door of hope' (Hosea 2:15). The discipline of God is always remedial. It is never to be despised and never to be rejected. It is designed to be a door of hope!

Questions

1. In view of God's statement: 'I will not be with you any more' (Joshua 7:12), how can we be assured that God is with us in power? Compare 2 Chronicles 15:2 with 2 Chronicles 30:6.
2. What does the story of Achan tell us about dealing with sin in

the church? Discuss the practicalities of Matthew 5:23–24, and Matthew 18:15–17. How do you understand 1 Corinthians 5:4–5 (compare 1 Timothy 1:20)?

3. 'I will make the Valley of Achor a door of hope' (Hosea 2:15) Think of ways in which God's punishment becomes a 'door of hope'. Share any personal experience you may have of this. Compare Hebrews 12:7–11.

Making decisions Old Testament-style

God had given instructions for discerning his will in important decisions when he gave orders for Aaron to carry the Urim and Thummim in the breastplate over his heart whenever he entered the tabernacle (Exodus 28:30). 'Thus Aaron will always bear the means of making decisions for the Israelites over his heart before the LORD' (Exodus 28:30). Exact details of how this worked are not given and therefore we can only speculate. However, the casting of lots may be a simplified version of this and it figures in the book of Joshua. It may have been the means of God revealing the identity of Achan after the defeat at Ai, and it was certainly an important factor in the distribution of the land in Canaan amongst the tribal groups: 'Their inheritances were assigned by lot . . . as the LORD had commanded through Moses' (Joshua 14:2). This practice continued throughout the Old Testament era (for example see Micah 2:4–5) and into the New Testament to the final pre-Pentecost act where a successor to Judas was chosen by lot (Acts 1:21–26). The principle behind this is explained in the book of Proverbs: 'The lot is cast into the lap, but its every decision is from the LORD' (Proverbs 16:33). It might sound to us as arbitrary as tossing a coin, but God had undertaken to direct the lot.

The destruction of Ai

**Achan's sin has been dealt with and Israel's
relationship with God restored. He promises
that they will now destroy Ai, instructs them
in their tactics and the battle takes place.**

The sin of Achan is dealt with and God and
Joshua are back on the original terms again.
The victory over Ai is already past tense in
God's vocabulary: 'I have delivered into your
hands the king of Ai' (verse 1). This principle runs through
Scripture. God's people do not fight to obtain victory, but to
demonstrate a victory already won (for example, see: Joshua 2:9;
Judges 3:28; 4:17; 7:14–15. Compare 1 Corinthians 15:57). For the
victory to be already God's does not eliminate the need to fight,
but it is to fight in confidence of the outcome.

This time Joshua is instructed to take the 'whole army' rather
than the 'two or three thousand' recommended by the spies
previously. The command is to '. . . do to Ai and its king as you
did to Jericho and its king' (verse 2), with one difference. This
time they may keep the plunder for themselves.

A battle already won

The plan was that 30,000 of the soldiers would set an ambush
behind Ai while Joshua and the rest of the army would advance
on the city.

When the king of Ai saw the Israelites' challenge he responded
to it by marshalling his army and hurrying out to meet them
straight away, 'early in the morning' (verse 14). Joshua and his

men pretended to retreat and fled back the way they had come, 'towards the desert'. So great was their confidence, that all the men of Ai were called to join in the anticipated slaughter of Israel: 'Not a man remained in Ai or Bethel who did not go after Israel. They left the city open and went in pursuit of Israel' (verse 17).

At the right time God gave his order to Joshua to hold his javelin towards Ai. This was a sign to the men waiting in the ambush who rose quickly from their positions, rushed to the city, entered and captured it before setting it on fire. The men of Ai looked back, saw the smoke and realized they had been tricked as the Israelites they were pursuing turned to face them. The 5,000 men who had been in hiding now began to pursue them from behind, surrounding the people of Ai on both sides. In the ensuing fight, every citizen of Ai was killed, with the exception of the king who was kept alive and brought to Joshua. The army then returned to the city of Ai killing any who were left alive there. Altogether 12,000 men and women were killed that day. The Israelites then took for themselves the livestock and plunder of the city, being very careful, after their experience of Achan in Jericho, to do it 'as the LORD instructed Joshua' (verse 27).

The sign of the javelin

Joshua had been holding his javelin out during all the fighting, which was reminiscent of Moses holding his staff as Joshua fought the Amalekites (Exodus 17:8–16). When the fighting was over he hanged the king of Ai on a tree outside the city, which was now a heap of ruins, then took him down to bury him under a large pile of rocks which they raised over his body in the city gate, 'which remains to this day' (verse 29). The public humiliation and killing of the king vividly portrayed the defeat of his people. The hanging of his body on a tree demonstrated the curse under which they had fallen for '. . . anyone who is hung on a tree is under God's curse' (Deuteronomy 21:23).

Joshua demonstrated a great principle in the whole encounter with Ai. Fighting by their own resources after the sin of Achan, the Israelites were fighting a battle already lost: 'I will not be with you any more . . . You cannot stand against your enemies' (7:12–13). Now, with his raised javelin in his hand, Joshua appropriating the power of God on their behalf, they were fighting a battle already won. God had promised Joshua: 'Hold out toward Ai the javelin that is in your hand, for into your hand I will deliver the city' (verse 18), for 'The LORD your God will give it into your hand' (verse 7). This remains an abiding principle of spiritual life. Appropriate the victory that belongs to Christ and we fight a battle already won. Live by our own resources and we fight a battle already lost, as was demonstrated when Israel lost their initial battle with Ai (Joshua 7).

Questions

1. The raised javelin in Joshua's hand symbolized the victory God had placed into his hands (see Joshua 8:18, 26). How do we appropriate in daily experience the victory won by Jesus Christ when he 'put everything under his feet' (1 Corinthians 15:27)?
2. In the light of his first failure in battle with Ai, on what grounds can Joshua accept the promise, 'Do not be afraid'? How may this be applied in our circumstances?
3. If Joshua can be described as 'fighting a battle already won' how do we work out the same principle in Christian living?

Joshua 8:30–35

The renewal of the covenant

Following the second battle at Ai Joshua builds an altar to God on Mount Ebal and renews the covenant with him.

After the victory over Ai, the chapter concludes with Joshua building an altar to the Lord on Mount Ebal, about 30 miles north of the approximate site of Ai. How much time  has lapsed between the defeat of Ai and this event we cannot be sure. Whether Israel had to fight their way through hostile territory to Mount Ebal we have no record. Perhaps the destruction of Ai put such fear into the surrounding communities (cf. 5:1) that they did not interfere with Israel. Clearly the whole nation is together, including women, children and the aliens that lived with them (verse 35). They have moved on from the plains of Jericho where they had launched their attack on Ai.

The altar as a focus

The setting up of the altar was by command of Moses (verse 31; see Deuteronomy 27:2–8). The purpose was threefold:

- to offer burnt offerings and fellowship offerings (verse 31);

- to inscribe a copy of the law God had given Moses (verse 32); and

- to pronounce the blessings and cursings contained in the law (verse 34).

The altar itself was built of 'uncut stones on which no iron tool had been used' (verse 31). This is as God specified to Moses on Mount Sinai (Exodus 20:25) and repeated when Moses gave instructions to the elders of Israel to build an altar once they had crossed the Jordan and come to Mount Ebal (Deuteronomy 27:5). Various views about this have been expressed. Perhaps 'the uncut stone represented the earth as God had created it; any attempt to improve God's creation would profane it' (Paul P. Enns, *Joshua* (Bible Study Commentary series, Zondervan, 1981).

Surrender to God

The two offerings, the burnt offering and the fellowship offering were both voluntary offerings (Leviticus 1:1–17; 3:1–17). They had been offered together on Mount Sinai when the law was first given to Israel (Exodus 20:24), thus reinforcing the solemnity of this act of renewal on Mount Ebal.

The burnt offering symbolized the surrender of the entire person to the Lord, though in this case it was the entire nation. The fellowship offering, as its name suggests, symbolized the enjoyment of fellowship with God. The offerer and God were working, living and functioning in harmony together. The combination of these two offerings therefore was a demonstration of a wholehearted surrender to the will of God, and an enjoyment of the presence and power of God which alone would enable them to fulfil his will.

The law engraved

The second event at this altar was the copying on stone of the law of Moses. To make this easier, Moses had left instructions that the stones should be coated with plaster (Deuteronomy 27:2). Engraving on plaster would be much easier and quicker than chiselling the words on to actual stone as God had done on Sinai (Deuteronomy 10:1–5). How much Joshua wrote we are not certain. Some have suggested he wrote the major portion of

Exodus, Leviticus and Deuteronomy! That would involve a lot of stone and a lot of writing! It is more likely he wrote the ten commandments. They obviously had copies of the whole law of Moses already, for they could only copy down what they already had before them (verse 32), and the reading of 'all the words of the law' (verse 34) which followed would be from their original copies.

It was in this position that the third and last event took place, the reading of the blessings and cursings from the Book of the Law. The six tribes of Simeon, Levi, Judah, Issachar, Joseph and Benjamin pronounced the blessings while standing on Mount Gerizim, and the remaining tribes of Reuben, Gad, Asher, Zebulun, Dan and Naphtali pronounced the curses while standing on Mount Ebal (Deuteronomy 27:12–13). As the Levites recited to all the people in a loud voice the cursings, they were instructed to respond, 'Amen'. The reading was the cursings and blessings recorded in Deuteronomy 27–28. Joshua is said to have 'read all the words of the law' (verse 34), though Moses had instructed the Levites to recite the law to all the people.

The likely situation was that Joshua gave the command to those who read, and they acted on his behalf.

The valley between Mount Ebal and Mount Gerizim is in the centre of Canaan. In this strategic location this act was declaring the rule and law of God in the land. The covenant with God which gave Israel the land also affirmed their responsibility to live as God intended them to live. To violate his plans wilfully brought a curse, as they had recently dramatically witnessed in the case of Achan, but to obey his commands would bring them blessing in every aspect of their lives.

The burnt and fellowship offerings represented their willing allegiance to God. The law represented God's deliberate and good purpose for them. The blessings and cursings represented the consequences of their obedience or disobedience in that relationship. All were affirmed by the whole nation of Israel in this ceremony.

Questions

1. What do you understand by the 'Old Covenant' and the 'New Covenant'?
2. Discuss some blessings and cursings that may apply in the new covenant of the New Testament (for example; 1 Corinthians 11:29–34; 2 Corinthians 9:6; Ephesians 1:3).
3. What do you think was Joshua's purpose in leading the people in a renewal of the covenant already made with God? Do you think there would be value in a Christian doing something similar? What comparable way would you suggest?
4. How do public declarations of our covenant relationship with God enhance our witness in the world? Give examples.

Joshua 9:1–15

The Gibeonite confidence trick

The kings on the west side of the Jordan united together to fight the Israelites. But the Gibeonites trick Joshua and Israel into making a peace treaty.

Having conquered Jericho and Ai the Israelites consolidated their hold on the central hill country of Canaan. These conquests effectively divided the country through the middle. From this position they go on to conquer first the southern part of the country (Joshua 9–10), and then the north (Joshua 11: see Map 1 p. 100).

Opposition to the Israelites stiffens

As news of the conquering exploits of Israel spread the remaining kings, representing the various tribal peoples in Canaan, formed a coalition to fight and prevent their further advance. The areas from which the kings are drawn cover the whole country (verse 1); the 'hill country' being the range that runs north and south in the centre of the land; 'the western foothills' being the area that runs down from the hill country towards the Mediterranean Sea; and 'the entire coast' running as far north as Lebanon. The description, 'all the kings west of the Jordan', is a comprehensive statement covering every part of the central land except, presumably, the cities and territory already conquered. This planned joint offensive against Israel did not materialize; the southern kings were dealt with separately to those in the north (compare chapter 10 with chapter 11). Six nations are mentioned altogether here, one less than the list of inhabiting peoples given by Joshua before they crossed the River Jordan (3:10): the Girgashites are missing.

In contrast with the nations who prepared themselves for war with Israel, the Gibeonites prepared to make peace. Gibeon was a city about 8 miles north and slightly west of Jerusalem. The Gibeonites themselves, however, were a coalition of peoples from the cities of Gibeon, Kephirah, Beeroth and Kiriath Jearim (verse 17). They were also described as Hivites (verse 7).

When these people heard what the Israelites had done to Jericho and Ai 'they resorted to a ruse'. They were careful not to mention the crossing of the Jordan river and the defeat of Jericho and Ai. These events had been too recent, and to have declared them would have exposed them as being from the vicinity.

Israel listened and responded. 'The men of Israel sampled their provisions but did not inquire of the LORD. Then Joshua made a treaty of peace with them to let them live, and the leaders of the assembly ratified it by oath' (verses 14–15). There lay the failure. They inquired of the Gibeonites, but did not inquire of the Lord. They took time to listen to the Gibeonites; they did not take time to listen to the Lord. God had given to Israel the means of discerning his will but they failed to apply it. When Joshua had been set aside as the man to replace Moses, he had been given Eleazar the priest who would, '. . . obtain decisions for him by inquiring of the Urim before the LORD' (Numbers 27:21). He failed in this instance to do so. Joshua had been tricked by the Gibeonites, but his failure to consult the Lord made him responsible for what followed.

Joshua's mistake

The peace agreement assured the Gibeonites of their lives, for its main clause was '. . . to let them live' (verse 15). This was in direct conflict with the instruction to '. . . destroy them totally. Make no treaty with them, and show them no mercy' (Deuteronomy 7:2). Although Joshua was mistaken as to their identity, being genuinely convinced the Gibeonites were from a far country he thought he had the right to enact a peace treaty with them, for that had been God's instructions to Moses concerning any peoples or cities who were not among the nations or cities God was giving to Israel as an inheritance (Deuteronomy 20:10, 15–16).

Questions

1. It has been stated that the story of the Gibeonite deception is a warning to the church of God against the cunning of the world. In what instances do you recognize this to be true? Where and how does the world try to make inroads into the church?
2. Israel were deceived by the Gibeonites because they 'did not inquire of the LORD' (9:14). In what ways may we 'inquire of the LORD' and discern his wisdom in making decisions?
3. How should we discern and deal with seductive elements that would infiltrate our church?

Joshua 9:16–27
The deception exposed

Joshua discovers the Gibeonites' deception but cannot go back on his oath. The Gibeonites are forced to become servants to the Israelites.

Three days after making the treaty with the Gibeonites the Israelites discovered the truth. Their immediate reaction was to set out for their towns and deal with them. They did not  attack, however, for they had sworn an oath to them that they would not take their lives. Although the treaty had been wrong in the first place, having made it they were now obliged by God to keep it. This is borne out later in the days of King Saul who killed many Gibeonites in an attempt to annihilate them. Because of the oath sworn to them by Joshua God sent famine for three successive years on Israel in return for this violation of the treaty. So serious was the breaking of this oath that David allowed the Gibeonites to put seven sons of Saul to death in recompense (2 Samuel 21:1–19).

Making the best of a bad job

The main consequence of this treaty was the establishing of a Canaanite presence amongst the Israelites, something expressly forbidden by God because he knew that '. . . they will turn your sons away from following me to serve other gods' (Deuteronomy 7:1–4). To prevent this happening as best they could, Israel reduced the Gibeonites to servanthood, if not slavery: '. . . let them be woodcutters and water carriers for the entire community' (verse 21). This menial service was the customary role of aliens living among the Israelites (Deuteronomy 29:11). The Gibeonites accepted this position, and were grateful for it, knowing the command God had given the Israelites in Canaan was to '. . . wipe out all its inhabitants before you' (verse 24). At least they were to live.

God still at work

There are practical lessons that can be learned from this story. We may make wrong decisions but be obliged to live with them and their consequences. Later in their history the people of Israel made another wrong decision in demanding a king. This was not the will of God for them; he described their desire to Samuel as a rejection of himself: 'It is not you they have rejected, but they have rejected me as their king' (1 Samuel 8:7). God's diagnosis of the situation is clear. The demand for a king was a rejection of God. Later, however, he said to Samuel: 'Listen to them and give them a king' (1 Samuel 8:22). More than that, God himself chose the king for them – Saul. When Saul went wrong God chose his successor, David, to whom he later made the promise, 'Your house and your kingdom shall endure for ever' (2 Samuel 7:16).

In a situation that had deviated from God's will as far as his original intentions were concerned, God was still at work. The effectiveness of Israel in God's purposes may have been hampered, and there would be difficult consequences of their choice which God would not intervene in to remedy: 'When that day comes, you will cry out for relief from the king you have chosen, and the LORD will not answer you in that day' (1 Samuel 8:18). We may look to God to enable us to live effectively with a bad decision, once we have acknowledged it for what it is, but we may not be able to undo what has been done, and we may have to live with the consequences of our own disobedience or foolishness.

In his dealings with the Gibeonites, Joshua was faced with a new situation for which he relied on his own insights and understanding. He did not consult the Lord which he could and should have done, and the result was that Israel had to live ever after with the consequences.

Questions

1. Joshua was wrong to make a treaty with the Gibeonites in the first place, but having done so he would be equally wrong to break it. Think of some situations in which this principle applies today. If your church makes a decision you honestly believe to be wrong, what is to be your attitude to the new situation?
2. What is the position of the Christian who has disobeyed God and sinned with irreversible consequences?
3. What is our response to accusations from the world that the church is corrupted? How do you justify your response?

Joshua 10:1–5

The coalition of Amorite kings

The treaty the Gibeonites had made with Israel to secure their own safety aroused the anger of Adoni-Zedek, king of Jerusalem, who formed a coalition with four neighbouring kings to mount an attack on Gibeon as punishment for their treachery.

The initial defeats of Jericho and Ai by Israel after crossing the River Jordan had sent shock waves throughout Canaan. The Gibeonites had capitulated in fear of their lives and now  the king of Jerusalem is likewise alarmed. He was one of the Amorite kings whose 'hearts sank' (5:1) when the news first reached them. The response of fear to the advance of Israel has become a recurring factor in the story (see 2:9–11; 5:1; 9:3, 24). Adding to the alarm of Adoni-Zedek, king of Jerusalem, was the peace treaty which the Gibeonites had made with Joshua. Gibeon was an important city, larger than Ai and described as one of the royal cities. It was located only 6 miles north and to the west of Jerusalem, deep in the heart of central Canaan. It had been a stronghold in the central hill country, giving some protection to Jerusalem from any invading northern force.

The consequence of the Gibeonites' treaty with Joshua left Jerusalem exposed and vulnerable. Adoni-Zedek called together the kings of four other cities in the region, the kings of Hebron, Jarmuth, Lachish and Eglon. These cities all lay to the south or west, and within a radius of 20 miles of Jerusalem, but had become equally exposed and vulnerable through the Gibeonite action.

The strategic position of Jerusalem

Although Israel had made a treaty with Gibeon they had not physically occupied the area. Joshua was still based at Gilgal where Israel first set up camp after crossing the Jordan (4:19, cf. 10:6). The coalition of the five Amorite kings united their armies for an attack on Gibeon, primarily to punish them for their alliance with Israel and presumably to re-establish the strategic defence the city of Gibeon provided for the rest of the region. Adoni-Zedek, king of Jerusalem, was the instigator of the campaign. Jerusalem was already by this time the centre of political activity in the region. Its high position made it a secure stronghold, and, in fact, Joshua did not conquer the city at all during his occupation of the land. The tribe of Benjamin failed to dislodge its inhabitants, known as Jebusites, after being given the area to inhabit when the land was divided between the twelve tribes (Judges 1:21). It was never conquered by the Israelites until David took it and established it as his capital seven-and-a-half years after he came to the throne, some four centuries after the occupation of Canaan by Joshua (2 Samuel 5:5).

Adoni-Zedek was therefore in a strong position, but like the other Amorite kings he had '. . . heard how the LORD dried up the Jordan before the Israelites . . . and they no longer had the courage to face the Israelites' (5:1). The cities who joined him in this exploit against Gibeon were all occupied by Amorites. The Amorites are first mentioned in Genesis 10 as descendants of Canaan, the grandson of Noah (see Genesis 10:1, 6, 15–16), and were settled in the hill country of Canaan (Numbers 13:29), though they were more widely spread and not confined to the southern region from which this coalition was drawn. They were well known for their warring skills. Amos, looking back to this period, writes of them descriptively as intimidating people, '. . . tall as the cedars and strong as the oaks' (Amos 2:9). Together, this intimidating force moved up with their troops and took up positions against Gibeon to attack it.

Questions

1. Each victory Joshua won aroused a bigger and more complex response. How do you see this as a picture of spiritual warfare?
2. The coalition of five kings felt they would be better placed together in battle against Joshua than if they fought alone. Although this incident does not present them as a model to us, do you think there are ways that co-operation with other Christians and churches enhances our ability to fulfil the purposes of God in the world?
3. The church has been opposed and persecuted throughout its history. How should the church respond to orchestrated opposition? What are some biblical precedents for your answer?

Victory is the Lord's

Threatened by the coalition of Amorite kings the Gibeonites appeal to Joshua for help. God assures him of victory.

On realizing they were about to be attacked, the Gibeonites sent word to Joshua: 'Do not abandon your servants. Come up to us quickly and save us!' (verse 6). Having made a treaty with them, Gibeon could now call for the full force of Israel to come to their defence. Joshua had failed to consult the Lord in his first encounter with the Gibeonites (9:14), but now God speaks to Joshua about this brewing confrontation with the Amorite kings: 'Do not be afraid of them; I have given them into your hand. Not one of them will be able to withstand you' (verse 8). Again the principle we have seen earlier comes to the fore: Israel is not fighting to obtain victory, but to receive a victory already theirs, for God speaks in the past tense of having '. . . given them into your hand'.

The ensuing description of the battle stresses both Israel's activity and God's intervention. For God to 'have given' victory is not to eliminate Israel's need to employ a strategy and fight, but to do so confident of the end result. This is made clear several times. Joshua 'took them by surprise' (verse 9), but 'the LORD threw them into confusion' (verse 10). Israel 'pursued them along the road' but 'the LORD hurled large hailstones down on them from the sky, and more of them died from the hailstones than were killed by the swords of the Israelites' (verse 11).

God and his people work together

This principle of being 'workers together with God' (2 Corinthians 6:1) applies throughout the whole realm of Israel's Old Testament experience and the Christian's New Testament experience, and is vividly demonstrated again and again in the book of Joshua. Along with obedience to God's instructions, in this case to go and fight the Amorites, is an implicit trust in God to intervene and bring about the fulfilment of his will.

The principle of God and man working together comes out again in these verses in relation to intercessory prayer. Here are details of a remarkable event, where the 'sun stopped in the middle of the sky' (verse 14), to enable Joshua to complete the operation against the Amorite kings. The writer describes it as '. . . a day when the LORD listened to a man. Surely the LORD was fighting for Israel' (verse 14).

Physical factors in this account have given commentators reason to look for explanations other than a miracle of the suspension of earth's rotation upon its axis for a period of time. Some have explained it as a poetic description of a day not longer in time, but fuller in content, where things were accomplished in one day that would normally have taken much longer. It is true Joshua's prayer is a poetic quotation from the 'Book of Jashar' (verse 13), whose poetry is again quoted in Scripture on one other occasion by David (2 Samuel 1:18). It seems therefore that this was a reasonably well-known writing in Israel but we have only speculative ideas about its origin and nature.

If the prayer of Joshua is poetic, the statement, 'The sun stopped in the middle of the sky and delayed going down for a full day' (verse 13b) is not. To make the whole episode merely poetic is to declare it untrue. Various unconvincing ideas have been put forward, such as the idea that the reference of Joshua to both the sun and the moon stopping still (verse 13) points to a total eclipse of the sun, during which time Israel was advantaged in the battle. However, that ignores the sun not '. . . going down for a full day'.

Those whose starting point is reason quickly dismiss supernatural phenomena and this incident, one of the most amazing records in Scripture of any event defying natural law, is hastily disposed of. Those whose starting point is revelation cannot get around the clear intention of the writer that this is to be understood as a supernatural phenomenon. The writer concludes his description of this event with a personal exclamation: 'Surely the LORD was fighting for Israel' (verse 14).

Questions

1. The extermination of the enemies of God seems particularly hard to understand. How do Deuteronomy 7:1–6 and Deuteronomy 9:1–6 help us to understand the reasoning for such activity?

2. To believe literally that 'the sun stopped in the middle of the sky' (10:13b) is to believe something that defies every law of physics and logic. Is a belief in miracles essential to being a Christian? Why? How do you present this to unbelievers?

3. 'There has never been a day like it . . . when the LORD listened to a man' (verse 14). If you were asked by your church to put together a day of intercession, what would it include?

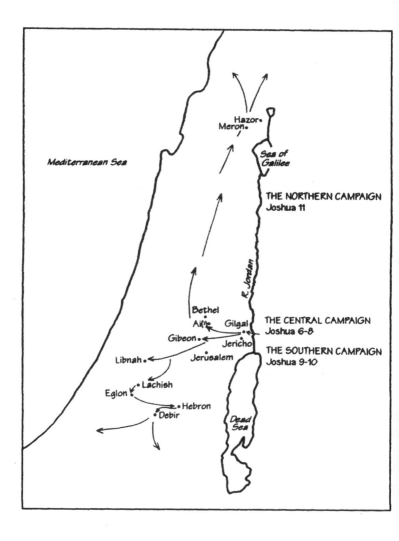

Map 1: The conquest of Canaan

Joshua 10:16–43

The southern cities conquered

The five kings escape and hide in a cave. After destroying the five cities and their inhabitants Joshua kills the kings then conquers southern Canaan.

The fate of the five kings is now described. They fled from the field of battle and hid in a cave at Makkedah which Joshua's men blocked with stones.

When the army returned, Joshua ordered the entrance of the cave to be opened. The army commanders put their feet on the necks of the kings and Joshua himself killed them one by one. He hung their bodies on five trees until sunset, when he gave the order for them to be taken down and thrown into the cave where they had been hiding. A large pile of stones was placed in the mouth of the cave making it the permanent tomb of these kings.

The Lord is conqueror

Placing the feet on the necks of conquered enemies may seem to the western mind to involve an unnecessary humiliation, but it was a traditional custom carried out by many middle-eastern nations, including the Egyptians and Assyrians, at a time of victory. Scripture speaks of God putting the enemies of his people 'under his feet' (1 Kings 5:3). David speaks of God giving him '. . . the necks of mine enemies' (2 Samuel 22:41 AV). In this connection it is interesting to note the imagery that the Father uses to the Son when he says, 'Sit at my right hand until I put your enemies under your feet' (Matthew 22:44 quoting Psalm 110:1). Paul uses similar language in describing the effect of the resurrection of Jesus when he declares, 'The last enemy to be destroyed is death. For he "has put everything under his feet"' (1 Corinthians 15:26–27). Placing the feet on the conquered foe is a symbol of the total defeat of the enemy and the complete victory of his conqueror. This is the language of the victory of Christ, its origin being in the military customs of the Old Testament.

The Lord's power is available

Having defeated the five kings, Joshua followed up his advantage and swung through the whole southern region of Canaan, attacking Libnah, Lachish, Eglon, Hebron and Debir, to the extent that, 'Joshua subdued the whole region' (verses 40–41). How long this process took we have no means of knowing, but the process was swift and it was sure. The judgment of God fell thoroughly on the corrupt peoples of the land and the whole of the southern kingdom was under the feet of the people of God.

One recurring idea throughout the narrative gives the true explanation of what was happening: 'The LORD . . . gave the city . . . into Israel's hand' (verse 30) and 'The LORD handed Lachish over to Israel . . .' (verse 32), summed up in the concluding statement: 'All these kings and their lands Joshua conquered in one campaign, because the LORD, the God of Israel, fought for Israel' (verse 42). The power of the Lord was demonstrated in the actions of Joshua and his men because the whole operation was '. . . just as the LORD, the God of Israel, had commanded' (verse 40). God's power is available for God's purposes, for the New Testament principle stands eternally true: 'The one who calls you is faithful and he will do it' (1 Thessalonians 5:24). Everything to which God calls, God enables. The relevance of Joshua's experience for us is to do as God tells us, in dependency upon God himself with complete confidence in his sufficiency and victory.

Questions

1. To place feet on the enemy is to demonstrate victory over him. Paul wrote of Jesus, 'He has put all things under his feet'. What are the principles by which I share in this victory? How does Joshua's victory over the five kings, after the Lord had said: 'I have given them into your hand' (10:8), help us to learn this lesson?
2. If the principle, 'The one who calls you is faithful and he will do it' (1 Thessalonians 5:24) holds true in this story, what areas are there where this same principle holds true in your personal and church life? How does this alter your approach to your responsibilities in those areas?
3. If God put all kings under Christ's feet (Ephesians 1:22), why is the world still in such a mess?

Joshua 11:1-5

The confederation of northern kings

Having conquered the central and southern areas of Canaan, Joshua turns his attention to the north, and its confederation of kings.

The opening statement of chapter 11 is similar to those of chapters 9 and 10. It was when the people and leaders of each region heard of Joshua's approach that they rallied together to defend their territory and to attack Israel. In each of these cases it is Israel of whom they are afraid. They have not yet discerned the presence and activity of God as the source of Israel's might, unlike Rahab describing the people of Jericho earlier (2:9), or the Gibeonites (9:24). Those who knew the fight was with God acknowledged they had no hope of success. Those who thought the battle was with Israel raised the morale of their people in the hope they would destroy them as they might any other advancing army. Those who looked at Joshua considered him destructible, but those who looked at God knew he was not. Israel's victory was assured because God was the source of their advancement and their strength. Failure to recognize this gave only the possibility of false hopes of success to their enemies.

Opposition hardens

Only the north remained to be conquered and its kings formed a confederation to resist the Israelites. Three factors were to influence the campaign: the strategic superiority of the kings, their large advantage in numbers and the power of God. By far the greatest of these was the last.

▶ Jabin, king of Hazor and ringleader of this alliance was undoubtedly the most influential king in the northern region. Hazor was strategically located about 10 miles north of Galilee and was the largest and best fortified city in Canaan. It was a key city on the trade route from Egypt to Assyria. Its probable population at the time was about 40,000 with a similar number of horses and chariots (Paul P. Enns, *Joshua* (Bible Study Commentary Series, Zondervan, 1981), p. 95). The location and status of Hazor enabled it to marshal other kings and armies together, with such broad influence that probably the whole area as yet unoccupied by Israel was united in defence of their territory and determined to reverse the exploits of Joshua.

Some of the sites mentioned cannot be identified with certainty, for example, Madon and Acshaph (verse 1), though most of the alliance involves kings surrounding the Sea of Galilee. The inclusion of some groups in the confederation is surprising. The Jebusites are normally inhabitants of Jerusalem in the south, though it is possible they had outposts in the north as many such details are neither explained here, nor known from other sources.

▶ The final size of the army was too numerous to count but was described as being 'as numerous as the sand on the seashore' (verse 4). They joined forces together at the Waters of Merom, a location about 10 miles north-west of Galilee, south-west of Hazor. This gathered army of the united northern kings was overwhelmingly superior to Israel, both in manpower and equipment. It was certainly the most formidable opposition Joshua had had to face. Humanly speaking, Israel would stand no chance of survival against such a force and the logical outcome was not only the defeat of Israel, but their complete destruction.

▶ However, God had taken into account the likelihood of such encounters before they ever entered Canaan and had made this promise to Moses: 'When you go to war against your enemies and see horses and chariots and an army greater than yours, do not be afraid of them, because the LORD your God, who brought you up out of Egypt, will be with you' (Deuteronomy 20:1). Now they were to discover whether God really did mean what he said!

Questions

1. The northern kings did not recognize God to be fighting for Israel. Compare this position with the wisdom of Gamaliel in his speech to the Sanhedrin Council in Acts 5:34–39 (particularly verse 39). How do you think we discern and recognize what is of God and what is not?
2. Israel would be able to recall the promise of God to Moses

(Deuteronomy 20:1) and face this huge army with confidence. Name some of the promises of God you recall to mind when faced with situations that would otherwise overwhelm you.

3. Recall some of the promises that God has made regarding our role and witness in the world (for example Acts 1:8; Matthew 28:19–20; Matthew 10:16–20; 1 Corinthians 1:28–31).

Joshua 11:6–15

The battle is the Lord's

The Lord tells Joshua not to be afraid of this new alliance of kings and promises victory for the Israelites. The northern region is subsequently conquered.

As Joshua faced the battle God spoke to him: 'Do not be afraid of them, because by this time tomorrow I will hand all of them over to Israel, slain' (verse 6). The recurring principle  applied as it had in every previous encounter on the battlefield: they were to obey God, they were to trust in his power and see him act. On the one hand, 'Joshua did to them as the LORD had directed' (verse 9), and on the other, '. . . the LORD gave them into the hand of Israel' (verse 8). Joshua obeyed, God gave.

Do not trust horses

Such was his confidence in the promise of God to hand over the enemy to him, the actual battle was initiated by Joshua, despite the superiority of the enemy's manpower and equipment.

'Joshua and his whole army came against them suddenly at the Waters of Merom and attacked them' (verse 7). They were instructed to '. . . hamstring their horses and burn their chariots' (verse 6). Israel had been prohibited by God in the days of Moses from acquiring great horse power: 'The king moreover must not acquire great numbers of horses for himself . . .' (Deuteronomy 17:16). The reason for this is made plain in the Psalms: 'Some trust in chariots and some in horses, but we trust in the name of the LORD our God' (Psalm 20:7). The horses and chariots were suggestive of physical resourcefulness and power. Although they would be used in battle by Israel, they were never to be the object of dependency or the means in themselves of obtaining victory. God was their power. He alone was to be the focus of their dependency and their source of victory.

To hamstring the horses and to burn the chariots of the enemy, as they were instructed to by God, was to strike at the means upon which the enemy had depended for their victory, and thus to demonstrate its impotency before God. The horses were not to be destroyed but hamstrung, that is, to cut its tendon above the ankle, the effect being to make the horse lame and unfit for war although it may still be useful for domestic purposes. Similarly, the command to burn the chariots was a command to destroy the war machine upon which the enemy had depended for their success. Any object of dependency is in reality a substitute for God, and therefore becomes an enemy of God and is good only for destruction.

Total destruction

The battle at the Waters of Merom was so decisive that '. . . no survivors were left' (verse 8). Having fought and won the initial battle Joshua moved on to take the prize of the city of Hazor itself. This was the most important city in the region, perhaps the largest and almost certainly the best fortified in the whole of Canaan. As was true in the other cities conquered by Joshua, he completely destroyed the inhabitants of Hazor, but then he burned the city to the ground, something he did not do to the other cities (verse 13). Hazor was probably destroyed in this way to demonstrate the conclusive victory of Israel over the mightiest power in Canaan, whereas the other cities were left intact so that they could be inhabited by the Israelites themselves in due course.

The Israelites were permitted to carry off all the plunder and livestock of these cities, unlike Jericho (cf. 6:17). The summary at the end of this section says: 'As the LORD commanded his servant Moses, so Moses commanded Joshua and Joshua did it; he left nothing undone of all that the LORD commanded Moses' (verse 15). Therein lies the key to Joshua's success. God had given him victory against all his enemies, but not in arbitrary fashion. It was in response to his obedience to all of the instructions God had given to him, and to Moses before him.

Questions

1. God tells Joshua not to be afraid (verse 6). This seems humanly unreasonable. How does Philippians 4:6–7 help us to be at peace in a situation that would normally produce panic?
2. Why is the average person afraid of death, usually seeing it as the ultimate disaster to be avoided at all costs? How differently do you think God sees death?
3. Joshua's treatment of God's enemies was to destroy them totally. What is to be our attitude to enemies and why? See Luke 9:51–55 and Matthew 5:43–48.

Hazor

In recent years (since 1953) Hazor has been excavated. Altogether, 21 cities have been found to have been constructed on the

rubble of the original city. One interesting discovery is a layer of burnt rubble indicating destruction by a great fire around the 13th century BC. Many scholars do not hesitate to attribute this to the destruction by Joshua at that time. That Hazor was rebuilt and became again a significant and powerful city is clear in the book of Judges. There, Deborah and Barak defeated 'Jabin . . . who reigned in Hazor' (Judges 4:2). Although this king carries the same name as Jabin, king of Hazor, defeated by Joshua, there are more than two centuries between them and they must not be confused as the same person. It is suggested that the name Jabin may well have been a hereditary title borne by successive kings of Hazor.

Joshua 11:16–23

Joshua conquers the land

The entire land, from the Negev to Lebanon and from the Mediterranean Sea to the River Jordan, has been conquered and taken by Joshua as the inheritance of Israel.

The final section of this chapter summarizes Joshua's conquest of the land. It begins rather matter-of-factly: 'So Joshua took this entire land . . .' (verse 16). Some geographical points are given: 'Mount Halak' (verse 17) represents the southern boundary, 25 miles south of Beersheba, a little further south than the southern tip of the Dead Sea. The northern boundary is identified as 'Baal Gad in the Valley of Lebanon below Mount Hermon' (verse 17), some 25 or so miles north of Galilee. Joshua was merciless in his occupation of the land, capturing and killing all the kings (verse 17), exterminating all the people (verses 21–22), and making peace with no-one except the Gibeonites who had obtained a peace treaty by deception (verse 19).

Does God harden hearts?

One of the reasons the cities did not surrender to Israel and so avoid bloodshed is stated: 'It was the LORD himself who hardened their hearts to wage war against Israel, so that he might destroy them totally, exterminating them without mercy, as the LORD had commanded Moses' (verse 20). The Canaanites were totally destroyed because of their iniquity, foretold to Abraham: 'In the fourth generation your descendants will come back here, for the sin of the Amorites has not yet reached its full measure' (Genesis 15:16). Now that their iniquity has grown to its 'full measure', its effects include the hardening of the heart, but God is not responsible for the initiation of this condition. When Paul writes of the progression of sin in people's lives he states that 'God gave them over . . .' to their sins (Romans 1:24, 26, 28), but in so saying, God cannot be held responsible for that condition. It was the consequence of their own attitudes and actions. The hardening of Pharaoh's heart at the time of the plagues is a notorious example. Although it is stated that God hardened Pharaoh's heart (Exodus 4:21; 11:10 etc.), it is also stated that Pharaoh hardened his own heart: 'When Pharaoh saw that there was relief he hardened his heart and would not listen to Moses and Aaron' (Exodus 8:15). The former is the consequence of the latter. The attitude of Pharaoh was hardened by the activity of God, but only because he was already in defiance of God. So it would seem to be with the Canaanites.

Are we ready for the long haul?

The destruction of most of the Anakites is specifically recorded in verses 21–22. Some escaped to Gaza, Gath and Ashdod, south-west of the country, but none remained in Canaan itself. They may be mentioned specifically because they were one of the reasons why Israel did not enter and occupy Canaan from Kadesh Barnea as they had been instructed in the first place. The spies reported that 'The people who live there are powerful, and the cities are fortified and very large. We even saw descendants of Anak there . . . we saw the Nephelim there (the descendants of Anak come from the Nephelim). We seemed like grasshoppers in our own eyes and we looked the same to them' (Numbers 13:28, 33). The Anakites were generally thought to be giants and it was in fear of them that the Israelites had been persuaded to turn tail and flee from any advance into Canaan on that occasion. Now 'No Anakites were left in Israelite territory' (verse 22) as though to set the seal of the victory God had given over all that which had intimidated Israel forty years earlier and prevented them from entering and enjoying the land.

The whole conquest of the land took 'a long time' (verse 18). The reporting of it in only six chapters of Joshua, after Israel crossed the Jordan river, may give an impression of the whole campaign being swift and brief, but apparently it was not. We can estimate it to have taken around seven years. In chapter 14:10 Caleb speaks of it being 45 years since Moses sent him from Kadesh Barnea to explore the land. That event took place 2 years after their release from Egypt, and 38 years before they crossed the River Jordan. If that event occurred 45 years before Joshua began to distribute the land, then they had been in Canaan for 7 years.

Questions

1. 'So Joshua took the entire land, just as the LORD had directed Moses' (verse 23). How do you understand the words of Jesus about the church: 'The gates of Hades will not overcome it' (Matthew 16:18)? What do we need to do to experience that promise?

2. How does the promise help us in evangelism?
3. Will the entire world ever be conquered for Christ? Pool your group's knowledge of the Bible in answering this question.

Joshua 12:1–24

Summary of the conquest

A summary of the kings defeated by Moses is given, with details of their territories, followed by a list of the kings defeated by Joshua.

Before Israel crossed into Canaan they had to attack and conquer the nations occupying the east side of Jordan. This had been done under the leadership of Moses, who took territory from 'the Arnon Gorge to Mount Hermon' (verse 1). The Arnon Gorge was a natural boundary running east of the centre of the Dead Sea. Mount Hermon was about 140 miles north of that, giving Israel a considerable amount of territory from which to invade Canaan, including the entire length of the Jordan river from Galilee to the Dead Sea.

Sihon and Og; symbols of enemies defeated

To conquer that territory Israel had captured two major kings, Sihon who ruled Heshbon in the south and Og who ruled Bashan in the north. The record of the defeat of these two kings is given in Numbers 21:21–35. Moses had requested permission from Sihon to pass through his territory without bringing any harm to the people or deviating from the main highway to drink from any well or eat from any field. Sihon refused permission and mustered his army to fight against Israel, only to be thoroughly defeated. Similarly, as Moses progressed north he met the obstinate Og, king of Bashan, who marched his army out to meet Moses and was also defeated.

The defeat of these two kings, Sihon and Og, became legendary, being referred to on about a dozen separate occasions in the Old Testament through to the books of Kings, Nehemiah, Psalms and Jeremiah. Rahab, in expressing her fear of Israel to the two spies who were hiding in her home, reported: 'We have heard how the LORD dried up the water of the Red Sea for you when you came out of Egypt, and what you did to Sihon and Og, the two kings of the Amorites east of the Jordan whom you totally destroyed. When we heard of it our hearts sank' (2:10–11). This defeat of Sihon and Og caught the imagination of people wherever the story was told, and had undermined the morale of at least the people of Jericho, making their conquest that much more easy.

This territory, east of the Jordan, had already been given by Moses to the tribes of the Reubenites, the Gadites and the half-tribe of Manasseh. They would return to occupy it properly in due course, once the land of Canaan had been subdued, but in the meantime their fighting men were actively involved with the other tribes in the occupation of Canaan itself.

The writer has included these exploits in his resumé of events, no doubt to demonstrate the unity of the land to be occupied by the twelve tribes. The land east of Jordan is to be equally part of Israel with the land of Canaan west of the Jordan. The generation might come when the eastern tribes would not be acknowledged as fully a part of Israel as those in the west and their inclusion in the record here might be given to prevent that. (Concern about this possibility is recorded in 22:24–25.)

Thirty-one kings submit to the King of kings

The writer then summarizes the more familiar details that have been reported in the earlier parts of Joshua. Thirty-one kings are mentioned as being conquered and they are recorded roughly in the order of their conquests and in which the events have been told in preceding chapters.

First there are the kings of the central region, Jericho and Ai, whose capture gave Israel its bridgehead into the country (chapters 6–8). There follow the southern kingdoms of Jerusalem, Hebron, Jarmuth, Lachish, Eglon, Gezer, Debir, Geder, Hormah, Arad, Libnah, Adullam, Makkedah and Bethel (chapters 9–10). One or two new names were not specifically mentioned earlier, Gedar, Hormah and Arad, but they can be located in the southern region of the country. Finally the kings of Tappuah, Hepher, Aphek, Lasharon, Madon, Hazor, Shimron Meron, Acshaph, Taanach, Megiddo, Kedesh, Jokneam, Dor, Goyim and Tirzah are all in the northern region around Galilee and the area extending to Mount Carmel (chapter 11).

The conquest of Canaan is now complete, and the stage is set for the occupation of the territory by the twelve tribes of Israel. The dominant theme throughout has been that God has 'given' (1:2) the land to them; that they are to enjoy their 'inheritance' (11:23) in the land of 'promise' (Deuteronomy 9:28) in a context of 'rest' (1:13: see also Hebrews 4). These issues are all developed in Scripture as essential ingredients in a satisfying walk with God.

Questions

1. It is good to reflect on some of the good things God has done and thus avoid taking his kindness for granted. List and/or discuss some of the blessings from God you have not consciously thanked him for of late.
2. The enemy is conquered but the land is not yet occupied. How do we experience and occupy the things with which God has dealt with on the cross and by his resurrection?
3. Suppose, at a later date, the tribes of Israel felt intimidated by

the remaining native people in Canaan, or by an advancing nation such as the Philistines. How do you think reading this chapter might be of help to them?

The Philistines

The Philistines make their only appearance in the book of Joshua in chapter 13:2 where they are mentioned as inhabiting one of the regions yet to be occupied by Israel. They are worth commenting on at this stage because in due course they become the prime enemy of the occupying Israelites (for example in Judges, Samuel etc.).

At the time the Israelites left Egypt the Philistines inhabited the Mediterranean coastline between Egypt and Gaza. Because of their occupation of that area Israel made a detour from the more direct coastal road to an inland route so as to avoid conflict with them (Exodus 17). In the ensuing years they have evidently migrated up the coast so that by chapter 13 of Joshua (when Joshua is described in verse 1 as 'old and well advanced in years') the Philistines have placed five rulers in the five cities of Gaza, Ashkelon, Ashdod, Ekron and Gath. Coming into Canaan almost certainly after the invasion by Israel, they seem intent on following up Israel's conquest of Canaan with their own conquest of Israel. This would account for their constant aggressiveness in the years following the account of Joshua, where they are constantly fighting for Israelite territory.

Time and again the Philistines provide the test case to demonstrate to a new generation of Israelites the power of God to retain for them the land he had first given to them. Men such as Gideon, Jephthah, Samson, Samuel, Saul, David and Solomon learned the power of God in their experience with the Philistines. It was only after 'Solomon ruled over all the kingdoms from the River to the land of the Philistines' (1 Kings 4:21) that the Philistines seem to have dropped the idea of occupying Canaan for themselves.

OCCUPYING THE LAND

Joshua 13–22

Land still to be taken

**The Israelites have conquered Canaan
(1–12) and now they settle into the land
(13–24). It is divided between the tribes of
Israel, though much remains to be claimed.**

The preceding two chapters have recorded
the successful conquest of Canaan: 'So Joshua
took the entire land . . . Then the land had
rest from war' (11:23). As far as the main
body of the land was concerned this was true, but the Philistine
corridor in the south-west remained untouched (13:2) and a
northern strip, 'all Lebanon to the east, from Baal Gad below
Mount Hermon to Lebo Hamath' (verse 5) also needed to be
taken. This territory extended as far as, and beyond, the city of
Damascus, to some extent on the edges of Israel's land, yet God
promised it and assured them: 'I myself will drive them out'
(verse 6).

This promise of God was conditional on Israel's obedience. He
had stated, 'If you carefully observe all these commands I am
giving you to follow – to love the Lord your God, to walk in all
his ways and to hold fast to him – then the Lord will drive out
all these nations before you and you will dispossess nations
larger and stronger than you' (Deuteronomy 11:22–23). The

relationship between obedience to God and trust in God lies at the heart of this exercise. The invasion of Canaan and its occupation has demonstrated that. The book of Judges, with its swings from oppression to liberty, from defeat to victory, and from weakness to strength, parallels exactly the willingness of Israel either to obey and trust and so enjoy the power of God amongst them, or to disobey and rely on their own resources and ingenuity only to find themselves defeated and humiliated.

Old, yet much to do

Joshua is described at this point as 'old and well advanced in years' (verse 1). We cannot be certain of his age, though a similar expression is used in 23:1 when Joshua is described again as 'old and well advanced in years'. He first appeared on the scene leading the army of Israel into battle with the Amalekites immediately after leaving Egypt (see Exodus 17:8–16), approximately 50 years before the time recorded here. Caleb, the only other surviving adult who left Egypt, is now 85 years (14:10), so Joshua is likely to be of a similar age, perhaps a little more.

It is good to note the contrast between 'Joshua was old' (verse 1), and God 'will drive them out' (verse 6). God never grows old and never gets tired! Generations are born, grow old, get tired and die, but God remains unchanged. Consistency among the people of God right through history lies in the fact that they are dealing with the same God on the same terms.

Conquest complete, yet much to be done

The seeming paradox of having occupied the land on the one hand, yet there being still much land to be possessed, is a true principle of the Christian life. The work of Christ is complete. Nothing can be added, yet in entering into his salvation we enter a process of constant growth. In coming to Christ, God has '. . . blessed us in the heavenly realms with every spiritual blessing in

Christ' (Ephesians 1:3). That is a present reality to which nothing can be added, for we are, 'complete in him' (Colossians 2:10 AV). However, we are to 'purify ourselves from everything that contaminates body and spirit, perfecting holiness out of reverence for God' (2 Corinthians 7:1). Because we have everything we need in Christ we are not now growing *into* Christ, for there is no more of him than that which we have already received. Nor are we growing *into* holiness in some evolutionary fashion; rather we are to grow *in* Christ and we are to mature *in* holiness.

Our position in Christ is secure and final, but our condition is a growing and ever maturing one. The land of Canaan is occupied, but it needs possessing. Chapters 13 to 19 deal primarily with the process of Israel possessing and occupying what is already theirs. This is a principle of spiritual life: we may be satisfied but never static, for there is always more. Children are born with all the life they need. They do not receive more life as time goes by, for the life they had at birth is sufficient. But they do need to develop and they will endure the growing pains that accompany that development. The potential that is inherently theirs needs conscious and deliberate training in order to mature into adulthood. Such is the process of spiritual maturing as we learn to possess what is inherently ours in Christ.

Questions

1. The land is possessed yet 'there are still large areas to be taken over'. If all the resources we need are ours in Christ (see 2 Peter 1:3) identify areas in your life that may still need 'possessing'. How do you appropriate the victory of Christ in these areas?
2. God said to Joshua: 'You are very old', then outlined the task that was left for him still to do. How do you think your church can constructively channel the energies and abilities of older people?
3. The principle that there are still large areas to be taken over

applies to the Lord's mission to take the gospel to the world.
What contribution can you make individually, and as a group,
to the task of world evangelization?

Joshua 13:8–14

The inheritance of the tribes east of Jordan

Joshua now turns to the division of the land between the twelve tribes of Israel. Nearly one-third of the book of Joshua is taken up in describing this process, an indication of its importance.

Joshua has to divide up the land of Canaan
between the nine-and-a-half tribes who had
not been allocated land east of the Jordan.
Reuben, Gad and the half-tribe of Manasseh
had been given territory on the east of Jordan by Moses, at their
request, before the Israelites had crossed over the Jordan
(Numbers 32:1–42; Deuteronomy 3:12–17). The land covered
the territory previously ruled by Sihon and Og (verses 9–13)
and was suitable for cattle and sheep, of which the Reubenites
and Gadites had large herds and flocks. The land was assigned
to them on condition they crossed the Jordan and fought along
with the other tribes until such time as the whole land was
conquered and the inheritance of each tribe entered into (see
Numbers 32:16–19; cf. Joshua 1:12–15). As already mentioned
(see comments on chapter 4) the women and children of these
tribes remained in their newly allotted land together with some
of the men to care for and protect them.

Half measures

The writer reports that although given the territory, these three tribes '. . . did not drive out the people of Geshur and Maacah so they continue to live among the Israelites to this day' (verse 13). The recurring trouble Israel was to experience in later years was directly related to this failure, not only on the part of these tribes east of Jordan, but also those of the west bank too. Judah did not dislodge the Jebusites living in Jerusalem (15:63) and Ephraim did not remove the Canaanites living in Gezer, retaining them instead as their slaves (16:10). The half-tribe of Manasseh on the west of Jordan did not occupy certain towns initially and, when they were strong enough to do so, did not drive out the inhabitants as they should, but instead subjected them to forced labour (17:12–13).

The consequences of this failure were not fully realized until the time of the Judges. The first question asked after the death of Joshua was, 'Who will be the first to go up and fight for us against the Canaanites?' (Judges 1:1). There follows an explanation of the failure of many of the tribal groups to drive out the Canaanites from their inheritance (see Judges 1:21ff). It was one thing for Israel to have conquered the land, but the initial conquest was not followed up by the occupation of every part of the territory. Little groups and communities of Canaanites remained intact, contrary to God's instructions. In some cases they were rendered powerless and apparently harmless, and put to use by the Israelites in forced labour. But they grew and they expanded and became a constant source of irritation and trouble to the new occupants of the land.

Privilege and service

Just one verse here is devoted to the tribe of Levi (verse 14). They received no inheritance of land because God was their inheritance (cf. 13:33; 14:4; 18:7). The Levites were the tribe to whom was given the responsibility of the care of the tabernacle and the priesthood. The setting apart of the Levites probably had its origin in the event at the base of Mount Sinai when Moses returned with the ten commandments to find the children of Israel worshipping a golden calf. Moses announced: 'Whoever is for the LORD, come to me' (Exodus 32:26), and the record states: 'And all the Levites rallied to him'. These Levites then went through the camp, armed with swords, and avenged the honour of the Lord by destroying about 3,000 of the people responsible for the sacrilege. In consequence Moses announced to the Levites: 'You have been set apart to the LORD today' (Exodus 32:29).

Their role was further developed in the laws relating to the tabernacle though the actual priesthood was strictly reserved, on penalty of death, for the Levites who were descendants of Aaron (Numbers 3:10). God likened the setting apart of the Levites to the giving of the first-born to himself, though Levi was the third son of Jacob, not the first (Genesis 35:23).

The Levites would have a privileged position amongst the Israelites, but they would receive no tribal territory of their own. They would, however, possess cities along with pasture for their cattle in locations throughout the land (Joshua 21; Numbers 35:1–5; cf. Philippians 4:19).

Questions

1. Some of the tribes failed to dislodge the Canaanites living in their territory. These became a source of frustration and trouble to Israel. How do you see this paralleled in Christian experience?

2. The tribe of Levi received no land, 'since the offerings made by fire to the LORD, the God of Israel, are their inheritance' (compare also 13:33). Do you think they had a good deal? After thinking of your answer, how does it compare with Luke 10:42?

3. The Levites were separated from the rest of the nation, not to isolate them but to release them for service to the rest. How

should we understand the role of the Christian as being separate from the world, without being isolated?

Joshua 13:15–33

Details of land for Reuben, Gad, and the half-tribe of Manasseh

Details are given of the actual boundaries of the three tribes allotted territory east of Jordan. This inheritance was a legacy of Moses' leadership, having assigned the land when camped in the plains of Moab.

The territory of *Reuben* was in the southern area bounded by the Dead Sea and the Jordan on its west. This had largely been the territory of Sihon before the Israelites had taken it from him following his refusal to let them pass through (Numbers 21:21–35). It was in this area, at Pisgah (verse 20), that Moses was allowed to look over the land of Canaan, knowing he would never personally enter it, and where he commissioned and encouraged Joshua to inherit the leadership of the people (Deuteronomy 3:27–28). It was also the area where Balaam was put to death (13:22). Balaam had been hired by Balak, king of Moab, to curse Israel, but instead God had turned the curse into a blessing (Numbers 22–24). Balaam was later slain by the Israelites when they took vengeance on the Midianites (Numbers 31:8), but the story of Balaam became a legend in the history of Israel (Joshua 24:9–10; Nehemiah 13:1–2; Micah 6:5).

The territory of *Gad* is described next. Its western boundary was almost the length of the River Jordan between the southern end of the Sea of Kinnereth (Galilee) and the Dead Sea. It was immediately north of the territory allocated to Reuben. A number of towns are mentioned as forming the perimeters of the area but there are no special features or historical links given in the description of the territory.

The half-tribe of *Manasseh* was also located on the east of Jordan. Ephraim and Manasseh were the two sons of Joseph. When Jacob blessed his sons on his death-bed, he told Joseph that these two sons of his, Jacob's grandsons, would become as Jacob's own sons, inheriting the rights and status that belonged to his other sons when they returned to Canaan. Consequently, Ephraim and Manasseh became known as the two 'half-tribes' of Israel. However, it would seem the half-tribe of Manasseh had itself divided into two separate groups at some stage during the wilderness years, and both were apportioned areas of land. The land allocated here, running east and north of Galilee included 'all of Bashan' (verse 30). The pasture-land of Bashan was famous for its ability to produce good livestock (see Deuteronomy 32:14; Psalm 22:12; Ezekiel 39:18) and also famous for its lush vegetation (Isaiah 2:13; Ezekiel 27:6; Zechariah 11:2). The rest of Manasseh were located on fertile land in central Canaan, west of Jordan (Joshua 17).

The concluding verses of this chapter stress that these arrangements were the ones decided and decreed by Moses. Joshua had no power of veto over them, so the plans already made are stipulated and implemented before the rest of the land is divided amongst the remaining tribes.

Questions

1. The territories of Reuben, Gad and the half-tribe of Manasseh had been assigned them by Moses (verses 15, 24, 29, 32). Joshua had no veto over that arrangement. What should be our

attitude to decisions and practices within the church that come from an earlier generation?

2. Why is it stated specifically that 'The Israelites put to the sword Balaam son of Beor, who practised divination'? Do you think he deserved that (see Numbers 22–24)? Why? What is the Bible's view of divination?

Joshua 14:1-5
Dividing up the land west of Jordan

The method used to allocate the land west of Jordan to the remaining tribes, according to God's commands to Moses.

Joshua, Eleazar the priest and the heads of the tribes of Israel were responsible for the division of the land. Moses had already stipulated certain conditions. He had declared the boundaries of Canaan (Numbers 34), the procedure of dividing the land by the casting of lots (Numbers 34:13), and had specified the names of the leaders representing each tribe who would oversee the process along with Eleazar and Joshua (Numbers 34:16–29). The casting of lots and the finality of the decision reached, left no room for argument or negotiation if another piece of land was preferred by any tribe (see *Making decisions Old Testament-style*, p. 82).

There is a practical lesson for us behind the principles governing the division of the land. It is that God chooses our inheritance. He has different roles for each of us and, although we may be tempted to consider someone else's lot as more desirable than our own, our roles are of his choosing (1 Corinthians 12:18).

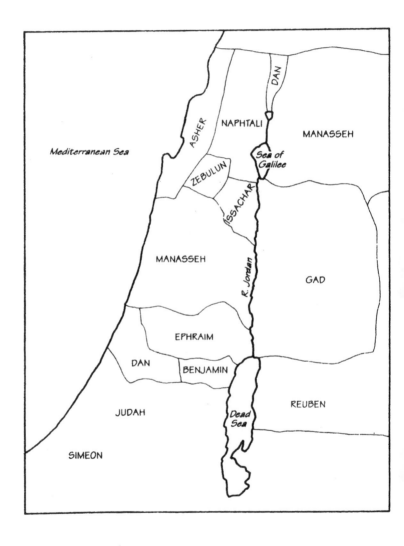

Map 2: The tribal divisions of Canaan

David wrote, 'LORD, you have assigned my portion and my cup; you have made my lot secure. The boundary lines have fallen for me in pleasant places; surely I have a delightful inheritance' (Psalm 16:5–6). There may be factors in our lives we would not have chosen, but God laid the boundary lines and in them we can be sure he is able to do his work, and we may rest secure in that fact.

The writer repeats the information that the two-and-a-half tribes have been given territory east of Jordan, and the remaining nine-and-a-half on the west, this time explaining that the two sons of Joseph, Manasseh and Ephraim, became the two half-tribes instead of the one tribe of Joseph. Reuben had been Jacob's first-born son, but had forfeited the rights to a double inheritance that accompany that position by sinning against his father (Genesis 35:22; 49:3–4). Jacob gave the blessing of the first-born to Joseph, the eldest child of his second wife, thus elevating his two sons to the position of being head of one tribe each. This makes a total of thirteen tribal groupings, although only twelve will receive land. He repeats the fact that the Levites receive no allotted territory, but only towns in which to live (see chapter 21).

Questions

1. The territory assigned to each tribe is described as an 'inheritance' (see Joshua 14:2–3, 9, 13–14). The word is used 45 times from chapter 13 onwards. How does this help you understand the idea of our 'inheritance' in Christ (Ephesians 1:13–14) and of his 'inheritance' in us (Ephesians 1:18)?
2. How would you apply this same concept of 'inheritance' to yourself, as in Psalm 16:5–6, and Isaiah 61:7? How would God's instruction to Joshua in chapter 1:6 help us to appropriate our inheritance?
3. In what ways has God sovereignly chosen the boundaries of our lives? How should this condition our attitude to difficulties we feel able to do little about?

Joshua 14:6–15

Caleb – the strong man at eighty-five

Caleb, appearing for the first time in the book of Joshua, claims his inheritance, promised him by Moses as a reward for his faith.

The first tribe to be allowed territory on the west bank of the Jordan was Judah. Moses had named Caleb, son of Jephunneh, to be the representative leader of that tribe; but  before the tribal territory is settled Caleb stakes his personal claim to an inheritance for which he had waited 45 years. As already mentioned he, along with Joshua, had been amongst the twelve spies sent into Canaan from Kadesh Barnea two years after leaving Egypt.

Ten of the spies had said it was impossible to take Canaan on account of the power of its five inhabiting nations, the fortification of its cities, and the giants, descendants of Anak, who roamed the land (Numbers 13:26–29). Caleb had spoken up to say the land could be taken, but the ten responded, 'We can't attack those people; they are stronger than we are' (Numbers 13:31). The spies' report was so demoralizing that the Israelites rebelled against Moses, wanting to choose a new leader and return to Egypt. Caleb was described by God at that time as being a man who had '. . . a different spirit and follows me wholeheartedly' (Numbers 14:24). Joshua shared his confidence that it was not the Israelites who would overthrow the Canaanites, but God. Their might was not in their own materials or methods but in God's presence with them. They encouraged the people not to be afraid, for 'Their protection is gone, but the LORD is with us' (Numbers 14:9). The people did not take Joshua and Caleb's advice, and as a consequence of their rebellion the whole nation was sentenced by God to remain in the wilderness (see p. 24).

The forty-five year wait

Because of Caleb's faith Moses had promised him an individual inheritance in the land of Canaan (Deuteronomy 1:36) and Caleb has now come to claim it. He gives testimony to the fact that, although he is 85 years old, 'I am still as strong today as the day Moses sent me out; I'm just as vigorous to go out to battle now as I was then. Now give me this hill country that the LORD promised me that day' (verses 11–12). It is not just the challenge of the hills that attracted Caleb but the fact that the Anakites lived there, the very ones that caused the Israelites to be afraid initially. The Anakites were descendants of the Nephilim and were generally thought to be a tribe of giants (Numbers 13:33; Genesis 6:4). Caleb has waited 45 years to go in and take the area, not to demonstrate that he was strong, but that with 'the LORD helping me, I will drive them out just as he said' (verse 12).

Caleb was not self-confident; his was a confidence rooted in God, who would enable him to conquer the Anakites. His faith in God had not diminished since the days at Kadesh Barnea. Having said that, faith and courage are inextricably locked together. It is confidence in God that enables the person of faith to break through normal limitations and inhibitions. Caleb's prime question was not 'What is possible?' but 'What is right?' and he could set out boldly to accomplish it in the confidence that God would make it possible. Daniel wrote, 'The people that know their God shall be strong and do exploits' (Daniel 11:32 AV). This would be a suitable epitaph for Caleb!

Joshua did not give Caleb the hill country he was promised, but he gave him the city of Hebron, which was a prestigious city in the centre of the area he allocated to Caleb's tribe, Judah, about 25 miles south of Jerusalem, and less than 20 miles west of the Dead Sea. It had formerly been named Kiriath Arba after the Anakites' greatest man (verse 15), and it would almost certainly be one of the fortified cities of the hill country Caleb visited whilst spying out the land from Kadesh Barnea. The reason for the award of this city is stressed again: by Joshua '. . . because he followed the LORD, the God of Israel, whole-heartedly' (verse 14).

After Caleb took Hebron, the writer concludes with the statement: 'Then the land had rest from war' (verse 15). It is 45 years since Caleb had believed God would give the land to them when he explored it from Kadesh Barnea, confident they could rest in God's sufficiency for the job. Now, at last, he has lived to see what he then believed.

Questions

1. Caleb's statement, 'Now give me this hill country' (AV 'this mountain') has long inspired people to reach out for greater and tougher things. What 'mountains' might we reach for both personally and corporately? What would help us to grow confident of being able to do so? Compare your response with that of Caleb (Joshua 14:10–12; Numbers 13:30; 14:6–9).

2. Forty-five years passed before Caleb received the inheritance God promised him. Someone has said, 'God's delays are not God's denials'. How do we keep going when our expectation of God's will does not seem to be materializing?

3. Caleb received his inheritance 'because he followed the LORD, the God of Israel, wholeheartedly' (verse 14). What did Jesus mean when he asked his disciples to 'follow me'? How does this apply to the Christian today?

Joshua 15:1–63

The inheritance of Judah

Judah is assigned its inheritance and the boundaries are recorded. Caleb drives out the Anakites from his inheritance, Hebron, and his daughter marries a future judge of Israel.

The realization of a dream

The division of the land of Canaan, which perhaps makes tedious reading to us today, is the fulfilment of God's initial promise to Abraham some five centuries before. The land in which Abraham's descendants would live, and from which the promise had been made that they would bless all the peoples of the world, was a crucial part of the covenant God made with him. The return to Canaan had been the dream of Israel ever since they had settled in Egypt 430 years earlier (Genesis 50:24), and was the object for which God had rescued them and led them out of their slavery in Egypt. Moses had declared to Israel in the wilderness, '. . . he brought us out from there to bring us in and give us the land that he promised on oath to our forefathers' (Deuteronomy 6:23). Conquering the land was a necessary process, but the end product was to 'settle down' in the land, with 'large herds and flocks, silver and gold' and to be 'satisfied' (see Deuteronomy 8:12). The actual settling of the land after its conquest was that which fulfilled God's purpose, and this is the event about to take place.

133

Stubborn realities

The prominence of the tribe of Judah is underlined by their being the first to be allocated territory on the west side of the Jordan. Judah was the fourth son of Jacob, after Reuben, Simeon and Levi. Reuben forfeited his rights to the benefits of the first-born (see the comments on 14:1–5), and Simeon and Levi had been guilty of killing in anger, causing Jacob to decree they would be scattered and dispersed throughout Israel (see Genesis 49:5–7). This subsequently happened, the Simeonites becoming absorbed into Judah (19:1–9) and the Levites never possessing territory, though because of their rejection of idolatry at Sinai (see the comments on 13:14) the curse put on them by Jacob became a blessing. The elimination of the three first-born tribes left Judah next in line, and to him Jacob had promised: 'your brothers will praise you . . . the sceptre will not depart from Judah, nor the ruler's staff from between his feet, until he comes to whom it belongs and the obedience of the nations is his' (Genesis 49:8, 10). This statement anticipates the Messiah, and also indicates the prominence that is given to Judah and to its preservation.

Judah, the front-line

The land area given to Judah is clearly defined. Its northern and southern perimeters approximately parallel the northern and southern points of the Dead Sea, beginning at the mouth of the Jordan in the north and extending to a line taken from the bay at its southern end, and is large because Judah was the largest tribe. In the last census, Judah had 75,500 men over the age of 20 years, almost three-and-a-half times more than the smallest tribe of Simeon with 22,200, and over 12,000 more than Dan, the second largest tribe (Numbers 26). The area roughly covers all the land between the Dead Sea on the east and the Mediterranean Sea on the west (see map 2).

This piece of land shared borders with three enemies of Israel: Moab lay to the east, Edom to the south and the Philistines to the south-west. Campbell Morgan has written: 'The tribe whose standard was that of the kingly line, and from which that line presently was to spring, was to have its fibre toughened by the sternest discipline – constant watchfulness against the foe and long continued fighting' (*An Exposition of the Whole Bible* (Marshall Pickering, new edn. 1992), p. 98). Privilege and blessing in Scripture do not remove us from scenes of conflict, they give us front-line status, right in the midst of them!

Caleb in the headlines again

Verses 13–19 (repeated in Judges 1:10–15) continue Caleb's exploits. He has been given Hebron, in the territory of Judah, and has spoken of his desire to drive out the Anakites. Now he is as good as his word. It is one thing to say 'God can' as a theological proposition, but another thing to say 'God will' and assume victory before the battle has been fought (cf. 15:14 and 14:12). The Anakites were no mean opposition, but Caleb in his old age drove them out.

Caleb then marched against Debir. This city had previously been taken and its inhabitants destroyed during Joshua's campaign in the south (10:38–39), so we can only assume the city had been reoccupied prior to the settling of Judah in the territory. Caleb offered his daughter Acsah in marriage to anyone who captured this city, and it was his nephew Othniel, the son of his brother Kenaz, who took the city and won the wife! They asked Caleb for springs of water in the dry and barren Negev and he gave them the upper and lower springs. This Othniel came to prominence as the first judge in Israel who fought against Aram after 8 years of oppression and brought 40 years of peace to Israel (Judges 3:7–11). No doubt he learned much of his skill, boldness and dependency on God from his uncle who became his father-in-law, Caleb.

'Count your blessings'

A list of 112 towns and their villages are listed as occupied by the clans of Judah, in the Negev to the south (verses 21–32), in the western foothills (verses 33–47), in the hill country (verses 48–60) and finally six towns in the desert (verses 61–62). The detail may again seem tedious and even unnecessary, but as the old hymn states, 'Count your blessings, name them one by one, and it will surprise you what the Lord has done'. Every place occupied was a reminder of God's faithfulness to his promises of many years. The territory belonged to Judah because it had been given them by God.

The story of Judah's territory ends on a negative note. They failed to dislodge the Jebusites from Jerusalem. King Adoni-Zedek of Jerusalem and four fellow kings had been defeated by Joshua after their coalition fought against Israel following the defection of the Gibeonites (chapter 10). In the wake of that defeat the people had not been totally conquered and some had been able to return safely to their fortified cities. Jerusalem is strategically located for defence and its inhabitants were never dislodged until David captured the city 400 years later (2 Samuel 5:6–12).

Questions

1. Things are often better 'caught than taught'. No doubt Othniel learned much from the example and experience of Caleb. Who do you imagine looks to you to see in your experience a demonstration of the things you believe? In this regard, how would you rewrite about yourself Paul's statement to Timothy in 1 Timothy 3:10–11?

2. What do you imagine were the dangers of not dislodging the Jebusites from Jerusalem? What personal application can we make from this?

3. Blessing and conflict go together in Scripture. Can you think of the privileges that are yours in Christ, but which bring you into conflict with the world?

Joshua 16:1–10

The inheritance of the children of Joseph

Following the allocation of land for Judah comes Joseph's inheritance, divided between his two sons Manasseh and Ephraim.

It was by Jacob's decree that Joseph was given first priority after Judah. Although he had been his eleventh son, Joseph was the first-born to his barren, but favourite wife, Rachel. Normally Joseph's first-born son Manasseh would have received his inheritance first. However, in blessing the sons of Joseph, Jacob had crossed his arms to place his right hand on the second son, Ephraim, saying he would be greater than Manasseh and so gave him the first blessing (Genesis 48:13–20), which is reflected in the allocation of the land.

One piece of land was chosen by lot to be given to the sons of Joseph and its area is described in these verses. It reached from the Jordan just north of Jericho right across to the Mediterranean Sea, and was possibly one of the most fertile regions of Canaan.

Ephraim's territory was the southern part of that attributed to Joseph. The details given enable us to draw his borders, though it did overlap with some territory given to Manasseh (17:9).

As with Judah before them, the people of Ephraim failed to dislodge the Canaanites living in Gezer (verse 10). They did rule them in time and required them to do forced labour (verse 10), but the command of God was to wipe them out (10:40b), and this they failed to do.

Questions

1. Every inheritance given to the tribes of Israel had their recognized boundaries. How do we define our own territories of service and ministry, and respect the boundaries of other people so as to provide the freedom to develop and mature?
2. Joseph was given priority, after Judah, over his brothers. This was because he was the first-born of Jacob's favourite wife. This may not have seemed fair to the others. How do you cope when life seems to treat you unfairly?

Joshua 17:1–6

The five daughters of Zelophehad

A brief interlude in the record of the distribution of land to Manasseh occurs. Zelophehad's daughters, in the absence of sons, demanded a share of their father's inheritance.

The family of *Manasseh* had divided into two sections. Manasseh's eldest son was Makir (cf. 17:1 with Genesis 50:23), whose own descendants were the clan who became known as Gileadites. They had received the area of Gilead and Bashon east of the Jordan which had been allocated to them by

Moses (13:8–13). This additional piece of land, west of the Jordan, was for the remainder of the tribe of Manasseh, the descendants of his other sons, Abiezer, Helek, Asriel, Shechem, Hepher and Shemida (verse 2).

A claim based on justice by God's promise

In the middle of this account of the distribution of land, a slight digression occurs, which illustrates one of the laws of inheritance in Israel. A great-grandson of Makir, Zelophehad, produced five daughters but no sons. These five women came to Joshua and Eleazar to request an inheritance of their own amongst the people of Manasseh, and it was granted to them. The background to this story is found in Numbers 27:1–11. After their father's death the women visited Moses and Eleazar at the tabernacle requesting that they inherit his property rather than it pass, as was the custom when there were no sons, to the nearest male relative. Moses consulted the Lord, and was told these women did have the right of inheritance. As a result the law was changed to allow an inheritance to pass to a man's daughters should he die leaving no son.

Now that the tribes and clans were being settled in the land, these same five daughters came to Joshua and Eleazar claiming, 'The LORD commanded Moses to give us an inheritance among our brothers' (17:4). This account shows their faith.

The exercise of faith

Their concern to claim what they believed to be rightly theirs was exercised before the nation had crossed into Canaan. It was a claim made by faith in God, showing a clear confidence in his ability to bring about the occupation of Canaan which he had promised. There was no suggestion of doubt that they might not have land to inherit, for they were not only certain of God's intention of getting them into Canaan, but in his ability actually to do it. Having obtained from God what they wanted they came to

Joshua to claim its implementation, now that the tribe of Manasseh, of which they were a part, was to receive an inheritance in the land.

The lesson we can learn from them is that what God has promised may be treated as true long before it comes into reality. When the reality comes into being, the issues are already settled, the decisions already made.

The story returns to the division and distribution of the land: that given to Manasseh was subsequently divided into ten sections (verse 5). Five tracts of land went to the clans of Abiezer, Helek, Asriel, Shechem and Shemida, and five to the daughters of Zelophehad, whose grandfather Hepher is listed as head of the sixth clan, but whose inheritance apparently was distributed among his granddaughters in accordance with their request and with the command of the Lord.

Questions

1. Mahlah and her four sisters had long been confident of God's ability to fulfil his promise to bring them into Canaan. They had therefore made provision in advance for that time. In what ways does our relationship with God help us to prepare for the future?

2. Women evidently did not have the same rights of inheritance as men, but the five daughters of Zelophehad stood against this injustice and 'The LORD commanded Moses to give us an inheritance among our brothers' (17:4). Against what traditional injustices do you think the church needs actively to take a stance?

The boundaries of Manasseh

The other half-tribe of Manasseh are given details of their territory, but they complained it was too small for them. Joshua's response is to tell them to clear some more ground for themselves.

The territorial boundaries of Manasseh are listed in verses 7–11. Basically it runs north of Ephraim from the Jordan to the Mediterranean. There is some overlap with Ephraim (verse 9) and in addition Manasseh received six cities located in territory assigned to Asher and Issachar to the north (verse 11).

Compromise again

The Manassehites failed the same test as Judah and Ephraim before them (see 15:63; 16:10). They failed to drive out the Canaanites. Judah had failed to drive the inhabitants from only one city, Jerusalem. Ephraim likewise had failed to dislodge the Canaanites in Gezer, though they reduced them to slavery. Manasseh failed in a series of towns. In the course of time Manasseh grew stronger, but chose to subject the inhabitants to forced labour, rather than wipe them out as God had instructed them (Exodus 23:23–33; 34:11–16; Deuteronomy 7:1–6). He expressly warned them: 'Be careful not to make a treaty with those who live in the land where you are going, or they will be a snare among you' (Exodus 34:12). It was true that this procedure would take time, for God had said: 'I will not drive them out in a single year, because the land would become too desolate and the wild animals too numerous for you. Little by little I will drive them out before you, until you have increased enough to take possession of the land' (Exodus 23:29–31; see also Deuteronomy 7:22–23).

Ephraim and Manasseh have now grown to sufficient strength to subject the Canaanites to forced labour, but they have stopped short of complete obedience to God's command in this area. Perhaps they reasoned that the Canaanites were of more value to them as slaves than by being exterminated. Perhaps it seemed more humane. Whatever their reasoning it amounted to disobedience.

When compromise is disobedience

King Saul made the same mistake years later when he refused to destroy totally the Amalekites, along with all their sheep and cattle, as God had expressly told him. When Samuel came to him Saul declared; 'I have carried out the LORD's instructions.' When Samuel challenged him to explain the bleating of sheep and lowing of cattle he explained that these were the best of the sheep and cattle, too good to be destroyed, and kept for offering in sacrifice to the Lord. It was then that Samuel declared: 'To obey is better than sacrifice, and to heed is better than the fat of rams' (1 Samuel 15:22).

To veto the will of God by our own rational judgment is to be guilty of disobedience. Saul lost his kingdom over this incident, and the nation of Israel after Joshua's time would suffer for their slackening on God's instructions to eliminate the Canaanites from their territory. After the death of Joshua, the gods of the Canaanites, the Baals, Ashtoreths and other hideous objects of worship, were the means of provoking the wrath of God against Israel and bringing them into conflict and defeat from their enemies around them (see Judges 2:8–15). To disobey may seem clever and smart at the time, but the birds always come home to roost!

Complaints turned to challenge

The combined tribes of Joseph (Ephraim and Manasseh) complained to Joshua that they were so numerous, having been blessed abundantly by God, that consequently their portion of land was too small for them (verse 14). At the last census the fighting men of Ephraim were 32,500 making them the eleventh largest tribe, though Manasseh were sixth largest with 52,700 (Numbers 26). Added together they came to 85,200 which made them by far the largest grouping. Some of these were already located east of the Jordan, but nevertheless they complained about their allotted territory being too small for all their people. Joshua's response was that if their land was too small, they should go up to the forest and clear more space for themselves. Then they complained that the Canaanites in the plain had iron chariots and were much too strong for them. Joshua told them to get on with clearing the forested hill country for as far as they could see, and then they would not only have more space for their large numbers, but be strong enough to drive out the Canaanites from the area.

Joshua wisely indicates that if the people of God would get on with the job of possessing what God has given them, seeing the opportunities rather than complaining about the obstacles, they would discover that instead of becoming weary in the process they would actually become strong (verses 15–18).

Questions

1. Think of some areas where we may be tempted to be dissatisfied with the declared will of God, either because we do not understand it, or because we actually disagree with it. Look at 2 Corinthians 6:14 and Matthew 19:9.
2. Ephraim and Manasseh complained that their portion of the land was too small. What things do you tend to complain about? How would Joshua's advice help you?

3. Many things intimidate the church and cause it to feel inadequate (cf. Joseph's descendants: 17:16–18). How can we adapt
   Joshua's advice in a way that would enable us to grow strong?

Joshua 18:1

Setting up the tabernacle

**The distribution of the land is again halted
although seven tribes have yet to receive their
land. The Tent of Meeting is set up at Shiloh.**

During the wilderness years God had insti-
tuted ceremonial laws and rituals designed to
give people access to God. These involved
the establishment of a priesthood, the per-

forming of blood sacrifices and the construction of the taber-
nacle, a tent that could be dismantled and reconstructed along
the journey. Various pieces of furniture were placed in the
tabernacle, but its most important artefact was the ark of the
covenant, kept in the inner sanctuary known as the Most Holy
Place, and which represented the actual presence of God among
the people. When God gave instructions for the making of the
ark he said, 'There . . . I will meet with you' (Exodus 25:22).

Now that Israel had conquered and begun to settle in the land
the tabernacle was set up in Shiloh. Moses had instructed that this
should take place when God had given Israel 'rest from all your
enemies' (Deuteronomy 12:10). There is no explanation as to why
Shiloh was chosen, but the choice was God's. Moses had spoken
about '. . . the place the LORD your God will choose as a dwelling
for his Name . . .' (Deuteronomy 12:11). Shiloh was situated in hill

country nearly 25 miles north of Jerusalem, in the territory allotted to Ephraim. It was central to the occupied land, thereby providing reasonable access to the whole nation. The tabernacle remained in Shiloh until the ark of the covenant was captured many years later in a battle with the Philistines at the time of Samuel (1 Samuel 4). Later David brought it to Jerusalem (2 Samuel 6), but it was his son Solomon who constructed a permanent home for the ark by building the temple in Jerusalem (1 Kings 6). Some translations of Jacob's blessing of his son Judah mention the name Shiloh: 'The sceptre shall not depart from Judah nor a lawgiver from between his feet, until Shiloh come' (Genesis 49:10 AV; see also RSV, NASB, etc.). This is a Messianic statement to be completed in Jesus, but the Hebrew may be rendered, 'until he comes to whom it belongs' (see RSV). (See 'Shiloh' in J. D. Douglas (ed.), *New Bible Dictionary* (IVP, 3rd edn. 1996).)

The 'whole assembly of the Israelites' is said to have gathered at Shiloh for the setting up of the tabernacle (otherwise called the Tent of Meeting, the 'Meeting' being with God rather than a reference to congregational activity. The New English Bible renders it, perhaps more aptly, 'The Tent of the Presence'). This is the first of three occasions when the whole assembly of Israel gathered together after inhabiting the land. Here they gathered to set up the tabernacle. The second occasion was when the three tribes east of the Jordan set up an altar by the river which was misunderstood by the rest of Israel to be a sign of rebellion against God. They gathered at Shiloh and decided to go to war against these three tribes, but a satisfactory explanation was given and the conflict averted (22:10–34). The final occasion was when Joshua gathered the people to Shechem to renew the covenant and hear his final speech before he died at the age of 110 years (24:1–27).

Questions

1. God's physical presence amongst the Israelites was in the ark of the covenant. We no longer meet him in a physical building

(see Matthew 27:51), so why do we go to church? Do you think it is important?

2. The temple of God became in due course a place of outward form, but detached from spiritual reality (Jeremiah 7:9–15). How may we avoid outward form replacing inner reality?

The tabernacle

The tabernacle or Tent of Meeting was set up by Joshua at Shiloh (18:1) and remained there until the time of Samuel.

The tabernacle was elaborately built by Moses 'according to the pattern shown you on the mountain' (Exodus 25:40) and in it was placed the mechanism and the means by which God could be approached and sin could be covered. Its main construction was a rectangular tent measuring 45 feet long and 15 feet wide (15m x 5m) which was divided into two sections. The Holy Place occupied two-thirds of the space, and the Most Holy Place (sometimes called the Holy Of Holies) was the 15 feet-square ($5m^2$) inner chamber. Various significant pieces of furniture were kept in the Holy Place, but in the Most Holy Place was kept only the ark of the covenant, which was the most important piece of furniture and represented the presence of God himself (see *The ark of the covenant*, p. 48).

The tabernacle is of immense importance, being the dwelling place of God. Its chief value to us is to give us an indication of Christ and the work that he did here on earth. In itself the tabernacle and the regulations associated with it were but a 'shadow of the good things that are coming – not the realities themselves' (Hebrews 10:1). The reality is Christ, and in the shadows of all its rituals, regulations, priesthood and furnishings may be seen the profile of the Lord Jesus Christ.

Joshua 18:2-28

Survey of the land

Seven tribes have yet to receive their land: Joshua accuses them of delaying taking possession of God's gift to them. He instructs men from each tribe to divide and survey the land, then he will apportion it by lot.

The tribes of Reuben, Gad, Judah, and the half-tribes of Manasseh and Ephraim had each received their inheritance, but the remaining seven tribes had not yet taken theirs. Joshua reprimands them for this: 'How long will you wait before you begin to take possession of the land that the LORD, the God of your Fathers, has given you?' (verse 3). Failure to take possession of the land already given them by God is a result of being 'slack' (see AV, RSV etc.) or 'putting off' (NASB), and a cause for rebuke. The fact that God has given the land to Israel has been stated by Moses and Joshua more than 100 times altogether, over 30 times in Joshua alone. The act of God *giving* the land (verse 3) has to be reciprocated by the people *receiving* the land. This is not a passive but an active response. Although possession of the land was already accomplished as far as God was concerned (he 'has given the land'), it was still in the future as far as the people were concerned (they have to 'take possession of the land'). The principle behind this apparent discrepancy between thought and action often explains the spiritual poverty of many believers who have been given all they need in Christ (see Ephesians 1:3; Colossians 2:10; 2 Peter 1:3), but who do not experience it and enjoy it because they fail to take hold of it for themselves.

God decides

The instructions for taking charge of the land God had given them was as follows. They were to appoint three men from each tribe to survey the land. The people are to divide the remaining land into seven parts, then bring a written report to Joshua, at Shiloh, who would cast lots 'in the presence of the Lord' (at the tabernacle) to determine which tribe would have which piece of territory (verses 4–6). To explore their 'possessions' was a condition of enjoying it. The men obeyed Joshua's command and returned to him with their written description. He cast lots at the tabernacle in Shiloh and distributed the land accordingly. This was not an arbitrary division. The people had investigated, described and divided up the land, so they knew exactly what each piece of territory consisted of, but the final decision came from the Lord himself. Years later David wrote, 'LORD you have assigned me my portion and my cup; you have made my lot secure. The boundary lines have fallen for me in pleasant places; surely I have a delightful inheritance' (Psalm 16:5–6). It is good to be content with the lot God has given to us, knowing that whatever its features, it has been assigned to us by God.

The first allocation here was for the tribe of Benjamin. Their area was small, being a thin strip not more than 5 miles wide, between Judah to the south and Ephraim in the north. From east to west it was about 20 miles long beginning at the Jordan river and extending to Kiriath Jearim about half-way to the Mediterranean Sea. It contained 26 towns and included familiar cities like Jericho, Bethel and Gibeon, though it skirted around Jerusalem.

Questions

1. God's *giving* has to be matched by our *receiving*. How do we appropriate his gifts (see, e.g., 1 Corinthians 15:57; 2 Peter 1:3)?
2. If for the seven tribes to explore their possession is a condition of enjoying it, how do we explore our inheritance in Christ?

3. How do the instructions for apportioning an inheritance to the seven remaining tribes help you to consider methods of decision-making? How did God's role and the people's role complement each other? Was one of the roles dispensable?

Joshua 19:1–51

Inheritances of Simeon, Zebulun, Issachar, Asher, Naphtali, Dan and the personal inheritance of Joshua

The remaining six tribes of Israel are allocated their land by lot. Finally Joshua receives his personal inheritance.

Simeon's inheritance was within the borders of the land already allotted to Judah (see map on p. 128). They were given 17 towns in the south of that region. Simeon was the smallest tribe with 22,200 recorded at the census taken by Moses (Numbers 26), their population having dropped drastically from being one of the largest, 59,300, in the earlier census (Numbers 1). The reason for this seemingly inadequate inheritance goes back further than the decline in their numbers. The allocation, made by the casting of lots before the Lord, is entirely consistent with the curse given by Jacob on Simeon (and Levi) because of their violence, in which he stated, 'I will scatter them in Jacob and disperse them in Israel' (Genesis 49:7). The Levites rectified their position to some extent, though were never to possess their own tribal land. But Simeon remained under that curse. When Moses blessed the tribes one by one on Mount Nebo, prior to his death, he had nothing to say to Simeon (Deuteronomy 33).

▶ *Zebulun* received a small piece of territory in the north of the country, to the west of Galilee, about midway between Galilee and the Mediterranean Sea. It contained 12 towns, though none of them are particularly significant. The name 'Bethlehem' (verse 15) should not be confused with Bethlehem in Judah. The New Testament town of Nazareth would one day be within its borders.

▶ *Issachar* shared Zebulun's eastern border and extended to the Jordan river, probably to the point where it left the Sea of Galilee, though its actual borders are not mentioned. The area was fertile, particularly as it extended into the plain of Jezreel, and it contained 16 towns.

▶ *Asher* was given the north-western part of the country, reaching from Mount Carmel in the south along the Mediterranean coastline beyond Tyre in the north, giving it the lengthiest stretch of sea of any tribe. The whole territory contained 22 towns.

▶ *Naphtali* was given an area covering 19 towns in the remaining land west and going north of Galilee, bordered by the northern Jordan above Galilee.

▶ *Dan* was given property between Ephraim and Judah extending to the Mediterranean near Joppa. It was a rather small area in which 17 towns are listed. However, they 'had difficulty taking possession of their territory' (verse 47), and later migrated north and attacked the town of Leshem, occupied it and renamed it Dan (a fuller record is given in Judges 18:1–31 where Leshem is called Laish). The city became the most northerly town of Israel. Often the length of Israel would be referred to as 'from Dan to Beersheba' (for example 1 Samuel 3:20).

The personal inheritance of Joshua

The record of the division of the land into tribal territory began with a personal inheritance for Caleb and it concludes with a personal inheritance for Joshua. These were the only two men remaining to have left Egypt as adults, and the only two spies sent by Moses from Kadesh Barnea who believed God would give them the land (Numbers 13–14). Without doubt Joshua is the human hero in the story of the conquest of Canaan, yet he did not ask for a possession of his own until everyone else had been assigned their land and settled in it. The receipt of his own inheritance was a sign that the task of occupation had been completed.

The Lord had commanded that Joshua should be given his own inheritance and he requested and received the town of Timnath Serah in the hill country of Ephraim, his own tribal land (cf. Numbers 13:8). Earlier, when the people of Ephraim had complained to Joshua that their land was too small for them, Joshua had challenged them to go up into the forests and to clear more land for themselves (17:15). Now he took up the challenge himself and took a town that was in need of constructing, for 'Joshua built up the town and settled there' (verse 50) and was eventually buried there, having died at the age of 110 years (24:30).

This concludes the record of the division of the land into tribal areas. There were still some cities and towns to be allocated, but the land itself was occupied. It had been carried out by Joshua, Eleazar the priest, the heads of the tribal clans, and the casting of lots in the presence of God in Shiloh. The human and the divine had worked together for the fulfilment of that which God had promised and God had delivered.

Questions

1. The tribe of Simeon received no separate inheritance of territory, only towns in the territory given to Judah, because of the sins of their forebears. How do the sins of our fathers affect us today? Compare your response to the promise of the New Covenant in Jeremiah 31:29.
2. What does the allocation of an inheritance to Joshua, last of all, teach us about true leadership? Contrast the disciples' idea of leadership with that of Jesus in Luke 22:24–26. How would you apply this in your local church setting?
3. Share some experiences of the human and the divine working together. How do you tell one from the other?

Joshua 20:1–9

Cities of refuge

Now the land is occupied the laws of the land given to Moses at Sinai must be implemented. This includes the provision for refuge in the case of killing someone unintentionally.

The occupation of the land is now complete and the tribes have come into full possession of the land. God now provides for individual need in times of crisis. Laws for the govern- ment of Israel were laid down by God to Moses as long ago as their meeting on Mount Sinai. Specific penalties for specific sins were given. The most heinous of all is the taking of another man's life, for which God had decreed in the law that no mercy should be shown towards the killer: 'Life for life' (Exodus 21:23). To Noah earlier he said, 'Whoever sheds the blood of man, by man shall his blood be shed' (Genesis 9:6). It was the task of the avenger of blood to see due penalty was meted out to the guilty party in such a case. But what if the death had been unintentional? What if it was the result of a genuine accident? In such circumstances there was provided a way of escape. Six cities of refuge, three on either side of the River Jordan were to be set aside. If the man responsible for the death of another fled to one of these cities he would be protected from the avenger of blood, though he would have to stand trial within that city of refuge, so that his case might be properly judged. When the high priest serving at the time had died, the refugee would be free to return to his own home with impunity (verses 4–9).

The 'avenger of blood'

The 'avenger of blood' was the person held responsible for pursuing the murderer and putting him to death. There is no detail given concerning how this avenger was appointed, but he may have been the nearest male relative of the one killed, or a representative of the elders of the city in which the death took place. The job of the avenger was not to determine the motive or cause that lay behind the death, but to avenge the blood of the one deceased.

The cities of refuge were provided to enable justice to be done where accidental death had occurred. It has been reported by Jewish commentators that in later times the roads leading to the cities of refuge were always kept in good repair. All obstructions that might slow a man down were removed. Every river was bridged and at every turning in the road there were signposts bearing the word 'Refuge'. (G. Campell Morgan, *An Exposition of the Whole Bible* (Marshall Pickering, new edn. 1992), p. 100.)

The cities of refuge

Six cities are to be set apart as cities of refuge: three on the eastern side of the Jordan, catering for the three tribes of Reuben, Gad and the half-tribe of Manasseh, and three on the western side to cater for the rest of the tribes. The western cities are listed first (verse 7). Kedesh was located about 18 miles north of Galilee in the area assigned to Naphtali. Shechem was in the centre of the country, approximately midway between the Jordan and the Mediterranean Sea, nearly 20 miles west of the Jordan at its halfway stage between the Sea of Galilee and the Dead Sea, in the hill country of Ephraim. The southerly city of Hebron, 20 miles to the south of Jerusalem and 18 miles west of the Dead Sea, was in the hill country of Judah. This was the city given to Caleb (14:13), and was centrally located for the southern region.

The three cities east of the Jordan had been assigned by Moses when he allocated territory there to the two-and-a-half tribes who occupied it (Deuteronomy 4:41–43). Golan was the northerly city, located in Bashan, and served the Manassehites, Ramoth was in the centre in Gilead and served the Gadites, and Bezer in the south, 20 miles due east of the northern shore of the Dead Sea, served the Reubenites. All of these cities, both east and west of the Jordan, belonged to the Levites, whose cities were to be allocated next.

Questions

1. How may the circumstances surrounding the cities of refuge and the role of the high priest within them be seen to be a picture of Christ?
2. Does this section teach a distinction between intentional and unintentional sin? How can we tell the difference? Share examples of situations where motives appear to be mixed.
3. What does this passage teach about God's concern for justice?
4. How would we answer someone who said, 'I can't help doing wrong. I am a sinner by nature. It's in my genes.'?

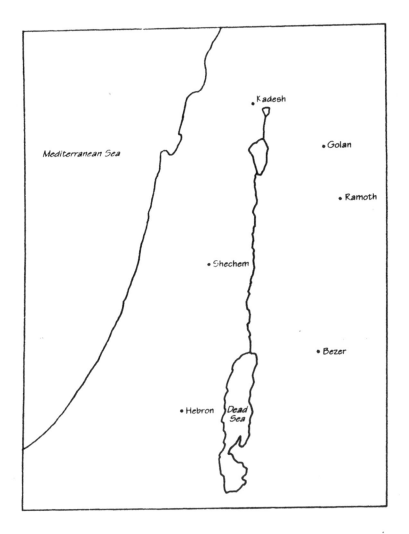

Map 3: Cities of refuge

Joshua 21:1–45

Towns for the Levites

The Levites did not inherit tribal areas for, in their priestly role, the Lord had declared himself to be their inheritance. They were assigned towns and pastures throughout the twelve tribal areas.

The uniqueness of the Levites has its origin in the fact that both Levi and Simeon had been cursed by their father Jacob, because they had tricked and then killed the family of  Shechem, a Hivite, who had wanted to marry their sister Dinah (Genesis 34). When Jacob called his sons to him before his death, he prophesied over each of them. To Simeon and Levi he recalled this event and said, 'I will scatter them in Jacob and curse them in Israel' (Genesis 49:5–7). As a result Simeon received no inheritance of land, but only towns in the territory of Judah (19:1–9). The curse on Levi had been changed into blessing as a result of the tribe rallying to Moses when he called for all those who were for the Lord to stand with him after the episode of the golden calf (Exodus 32:26; see comments on 13:14). The Levites are still not to inherit land of their own, as Jacob had decreed, but the Lord himself, involving all the privileges of service with the tabernacle, was to be their inheritance (Joshua 13:14, 33; 14:4; 18:7).

Privileges for the faithful

After all the other tribes had been allocated their inheritance the heads of the Levitical families approached Eleazar and Joshua at Shiloh and reminded them that the Lord had commanded they should be given towns to live in with pasture-land for their livestock (Numbers 35:1–5). Moses had instructed that in addition to the cities themselves they must be given land of a radius of 1,000 metres from their city walls on which to pasture their cattle and sheep.

Levi had three sons, Gershon, Kohath and Merari, from each of whom descended the three clans of Levites: the Gershonites, Kohathites and Merarites (Exodus 6:16; Numbers 3:17). The Kohathites were the priestly clan, being related to Aaron, the son of Amram, who was the son of Kohath (Exodus 6:16–20). The Gershonites and Merarites had responsibilities in relation to the tabernacle, but were subordinate to the actual priests (Numbers 1:47–53). All three branches were Levites, but only Kohathites were actual priests.

Method of allocation

The towns were again allocated by the casting of lots. The first lot came out for the Kohathites. Those of their number who were 'descendants of Aaron the priest' (verse 4) were allotted 13 cities in the southern area, from within the tribal boundaries of Judah (9 towns), and Benjamin (4 towns) (verses 13–17). The territory of Simeon is mentioned at this point, but their inheritance consisted of towns within Judah and they were not called to give up any actual territory to the Levites. Interestingly, these towns are within the closest proximity to Jerusalem where eventually the temple would be built, where God would cause his 'name to dwell', and the priestly role would be paramount.

The Kohathites not related to Aaron were given 10 towns from the tribes of Ephraim (4 towns), Dan (4 towns) and the half-tribe of Manasseh (2 towns), immediately to the north of their fellow Kohathites, but still surrounding Jerusalem (verses 20–26).

The Gershonites were given 13 towns from the tribes of Issachar (4 towns), Asher (4 towns), Naphtali (3 towns) and Manasseh's territory across the Jordan in Bashan (2 towns) (verses 27–33).

The Merarites were given 12 towns in the remaining tribes of Reuben (4 towns), Gad (4 towns) and Zebulun (4 towns) (verses 34–40). Altogether 48 towns were allocated to the Levites, the number previously specified by Moses before the nation had entered Canaan (Numbers 35:6). Six of the cities served as the cities of refuge.

The Lord's faithfulness

The final three verses of this chapter acknowledge the Lord's faithfulness throughout the whole operation, and crystallizes the message of the entire book. With everyone now settled in the land of Canaan, the chapter concludes with the satisfying statement: 'Not one of all the LORD's good promises to the house of Israel failed; every one was fulfilled'. Firstly the Lord had given the land he promised to Israel's forefathers (chapters 1–12). Then Israel had taken possession and settled there (chapters 13–22). Following this the Lord had given them rest on every side, so that the eastern tribes could at last return home; and Joshua could renew the covenant at Shechem, reminding the people of all God had done to bring them to the place of rest (chapters 22–24). The writer of Joshua can look back over this period and affirm that not one of all the Lord's good promises to the house of Israel had failed; every one of them was fulfilled.

Questions

1. The Levites experienced both privilege and sacrifice. Think of some of the privileges of the Christian life, and then of any sacrificial cost that may accompany them. Where does our failure to make the sacrifice deny us the privileges?
2. Try to rewrite Joshua 21:43–45 as your personal testimony.
3. The towns were allocated by lot. Are our circumstances given to us 'by lot', or by a supreme God, or do we earn them? How can we know?

The eastern tribes go home

The book of Joshua draws to a close with three accounts of the whole nation gathering together. The first, at Shiloh, marks the return of the tribes of Ephraim, Gad and Manasseh to their lands east of Jordan.

 As mentioned Moses had given land east of Jordan to the tribes of Ephraim, Gad and Manasseh with the proviso that first they must help their brothers conquer and take possession of the land west of the Jordan before they could settle on their own property (Numbers 32:20–22; cf. Joshua 1:12–18). They had left their wives and children in their land, but all the fighting men had crossed the Jordan fully armed for war against Canaan. Now that the land had been conquered and the domestic arrangements completed, Joshua called the tribes of Reuben, Gad and the half-tribe of Manasseh to him at Shiloh and acknowledged their obedience to the command of the Lord in not deserting their brothers until they had settled themselves in Canaan.

Before sending them off he exhorts them to '. . .be very careful to keep the commandment and the law that Moses the servant of the LORD gave you: to love the LORD your God, to walk in all his ways, to obey his commands, to hold fast to him and to serve him with all your heart and all your soul' (verse 5). This is reminiscent of Moses' instructions to Israel to follow God once they have entered the land (Deuteronomy 10:12–13; 11:22–23). Although addressed to the tribes returning to their land east of Jordan, Joshua's words would apply to all of Israel (chapters 23–24). Joshua's words express a fivefold outworking of the relationship of the people to their God.

They were to love the Lord

This lies at the root of all that is demanded by God of his people. Jesus summed up the law as being to 'Love the Lord your God with all your heart and with all your soul and with all your mind' (Matthew 22:37). Obedience to God must be in the context of relationship with God. To separate the demands of the law from the dynamics of relationship is to destroy their purpose and to undermine the possibility of their fulfilment.

They were to walk in his ways

Walking does not describe a position but a process. The boundary of their movement through life was to be the will of God, and every decision, every action and every intention would draw its legitimacy from its relationship to the divine will. Every step would be in acknowledgment of God. Solomon later wrote: 'In all your ways acknowledge him, and he will direct your paths' (Proverbs 3:6).

They were to obey his commands

The true expression of love for God is obedience to God. To walk in his ways involves trusting the direction of his Spirit. This may have different implications at different times in different lives, but the commands themselves remain consistent for all people at all times. They were written in stone and were non-negotiable. The specific will of God for individual people is never outside of the general will of God for all his people, and it is to this that his people, then and now, must be obedient.

They were to hold fast to God

There was no doubting that God would hold fast to Israel as their recent history had demonstrated. Not one of his good promises to Israel had failed (21:45), but the exhortation is now for Israel to hold fast to God. This they conspicuously failed to do in their ensuing history. Failure to fulfil their destiny or to enjoy God's blessing never had its origin in God's failure to hold fast to them, but always in their failure to hold fast to him. So it is in our own walk with God.

They were to serve him

The concept of service lay behind the unique relationship that Israel had with God. They had been chosen by God to be the means by which God would bring his blessings to the world. They had not been chosen for status but for service. God had said to Abraham, '. . . all peoples on earth will be blessed through you' (Genesis 12:3). This sense of servanthood was not to be lost but to be a distinctive feature of his people. This service was to be with '. . . all your heart and all your soul' (verse 5). This was to be no half-hearted affair, an obligation that could be attended to once in a while, but a driving passion evident in everything their hearts turned towards, and in every ambition of their souls.

Questions

1. How can we support those engaged in service for God that does not directly affect us? How should we divide our financial support between our own church and other Christian agencies?
2. Can you find equivalent instructions to Christians in the New Testament to those given by Joshua in 22:5? Discuss their implications for the life of a Christian called to live and work in a secular context.
3. Write, or suggest, what you consider to be five important things a Christian should do constantly to keep safe in a pagan environment.

Joshua 22:6–34

The altar built at Jordan

The two-and-a-half tribes return home east of Jordan, building an altar on the border. The remaining tribes, misunderstanding their intentions, gather a second time at Shiloh and discuss war against them.

Joshua sent the two-and-a-half tribes away to their homes blessing them with the promise of great wealth, large herds, silver, gold, bronze, iron and plenty of clothing. Material  blessing was a sign of God's blessing on Israel (Deuteronomy 28:1–14). The wealth they are to take home with them resulted from the conquest of the land. The policy determining the distribution of conquered wealth was given to Moses by God: 'Divide the spoils between the soldiers who took part in the battle and the rest of the community' (Numbers 31:27). The two-and-a-half tribes were to return home and 'divide with your brothers the plunder from your enemies' (22:8). Not all the men of these tribes had crossed the Jordan for battle. Some had inevitably remained behind to provide and care for the women and children, but they would get a share of the spoils.

The returning tribes left the rest of the Israelites at Shiloh, but when they crossed the Jordan river at Geliloth, they built an imposing altar by the Jordan, evidently visible from a great distance. Building an altar did not in itself imply a form of paganism or a rejection of the true God. Altars had been built by Noah (Genesis 8:20), Abraham (Genesis 12:7–8; 13:18; 22:9), Isaac (Genesis 26:25), Jacob (Genesis 33:20; 35:7), Moses (Exodus 17:15; 24:4), and even by Joshua (Joshua 8:30). In the case of Joshua, this was after God had given instructions to build the tabernacle with its altar upon which acceptable sacrifice would be made to God. Building an altar in itself may not be an illegitimate action.

When the rest of Israel heard of the construction of this altar by the returning two-and-a-half tribes they assumed it to be an act of rebellion and gathered at Shiloh for the purpose of going to war with them. Phineas, the son of Eleazar the priest, was sent with a representative of each tribe to meet with the tribes east of Jordan. He spoke first and listened second! He asked how they could break faith with God and build an altar in rebellion against him. He reminded them of the sin of Peor (Numbers 23:28) and of Achan (Joshua 7), and how the whole community felt the wrath of God as a result. He invited them to come across the Jordan and settle on the west side if their land was defiled, but at all costs they should not build an altar other than to the Lord.

Phineas asked for no explanation of the altar, only for an explanation of their rebellion. He assumed his interpretation of the meaning of the altar was correct so he launched into a tirade against them for what he thought to be their rebellion against God. Before any reply had been given he even presented a solution by inviting them to migrate across the Jordan to the mainland of Canaan if their dissatisfaction with the land was the reason for the rebellion. To his credit, he spoke before he fought, for all Israel was 'ready to go to war' (verse 12), but the assumptions that led to this outcry were to be proved wrong. There are practical lessons we can learn from this. To make assumptions about people's actions or motives without listening to their own explanation first can be dangerous and lead to misunderstandings with serious consequences.

The accused people replied that God knew the facts, and if this had been a rebellion against God then let them be destroyed. Far from being a rebellion against the God of Israel it was a token of their desire to maintain the unity of the nation and its relationship with God. With the Jordan serving as a natural physical barrier between the tribes located east and west of its valley, future generations might say the eastern tribes have no share in the Lord or his inheritance. The altar was intended to witness to the fact they worshipped the same Lord in the same way. The burnt offerings and sacrifices were not to be offered here, but at the tabernacle, and the replica they had built would serve to symbolize the unity of the tribes either side of the river for future generations.

When Phineas and the leaders returned to Shiloh with this explanation, the people were glad and praised God. They disbanded their plans for war and talked no more about it.

Meanwhile the tribes east of the Jordan gave the altar a name: 'A Witness Between Us that the LORD is God' (verse 34; cf. verses 27–28, 'It is to be a witness between us and you . . .'). To name an altar was not unusual. Jacob called his altar near Shechem, 'El Elohe Israel', which means 'God is the God of Israel' (Genesis 33:20), and Moses built an altar after the victory over the Amalekites in the desert, calling it 'The LORD is my Banner' (Exodus 17:15). Later Samuel did something similar after victory over the Philistines when he set up a stone and called it 'Ebenezer', meaning 'Thus far has the LORD helped us' (1 Samuel 7:12).

Questions

1. If material prosperity was a sign of God's blessing on Israel, may that principle be equally applied to believers today? What are the biblical grounds for your conclusions?
2. If we find some fellow-believer acting in a way that appears to be wrong, how do you think we should approach the problem – if at all? (Compare: Matthew 5:23–24; Luke 17:3–4; Matthew 18:15–17; Matthew 7:4–5).
3. Are there situations of conflict between people in your church or community where one side has not taken time to ask questions, to listen and therefore to understand the other perspective? If so, how should we avoid this kind of misunderstanding? How does humility play a part in breaking down divisions?

PRESERVING THE LAND

Joshua 23–24

Joshua 23:1-5

Looking back in gratitude

Some years after the events already recorded Joshua is reaching the end of his life. He summons together the leaders of Israel to remind them of God's goodness and to say farewell.

The period described as 'After a long time had passed' (verse 1) is not specified, but a lengthy interval has evidently taken place since the settlement of the tribes in their home areas. Joshua is even older (cf. 13:1) and if this event took place shortly before his death then he was approaching 110 years of age (24:29).

Leaders called together

Joshua called the leaders of the people to him, 'their elders, leaders, judges and officials'. In the following chapter Joshua is to address the whole nation, but here he speaks in particular to the leaders. This combination of leaders is mentioned earlier when the covenant was renewed at Mount Ebal after victory over Ai (8:33).

The 'elders' would seem to be the experienced and wise men who oversaw the local community life, as in 'the elders of the city' (20:4). The 'leaders' (in some translations 'heads' or 'chiefs') had a position of tribal authority (22:14), as in 'heads of the clans of Israel' (22:30). The judges administered justice as their name implies. They are only mentioned elsewhere in Joshua in 8:33, though their position in Joshua should not be confused with the role of those of the same name in the book of Judges. Finally the 'officials' would seem to have functioned like our policemen (for example, 'The officers went throughout the camp giving orders to the people,' 3:2). These men, all with tribal, city or community authority, were summoned to hear a final word from the man who held authority over them all.

He begins by reminding them that their recent history is a story of divine activity: 'You yourselves have seen everything the LORD your God has done' (verse 3). The conquest of the land was not something Israel had done for God, but something God had done for Israel: 'it was the LORD your God who fought for you' (verse 3). Their settled presence in the land could have no other legitimate explanation than its being achieved by the presence and power of God. It is always good to be reminded of the indispensability of God's activity to the process that enables us to fulfil his will. The New Testament principle, 'The one who calls you is faithful and he will do it' (1 Thessalonians 5:24) applies here.

Israel had been called to acts of obedience, the conquering of the land had been achieved through their physical activity, but behind it all was the activity of God. However, the work of God was not to the exclusion of the people. Joshua speaks of 'The LORD your God who fought for you' on the one hand, and of 'the nations I conquered' on the other. Although it is God who was at work, his work was not independent of the people, but it was through the people. Paul combines the two elements when he speaks of being 'God's fellow-workers' (2 Corinthians 6:1). Later Joshua says, 'One of you routs a thousand, because the LORD your God fights for you' (verse 10). These leaders therefore are reminded of the indispensability of God to the work, but of the equal necessity of their obedience in the process.

God's help for the future

There is still more work to be done. Joshua reminds them how the land was conquered between the Jordan and the Mediterranean Sea, how he then divided the land between the tribes into their separate inheritance, but how some remaining people still need to be driven out and the land fully appropriated. Their confidence in this being accomplished was to be placed in the Lord. 'He will push them out before you, and you will take possession of their land' (verse 5).

Four times in these verses Joshua refers to 'The LORD your God'. This description combines the objective with the subjective. Having pointed out that they have seen God demonstrate his miraculous power in giving them the land against overwhelming human impossibilities, this God is not detached and remote from their personal lives, but one with whom they have personal dealings and personal relationship. He is 'your God'. This precipitates the personal instructions that are to follow which will keep the terms of the relationship intact.

Questions

1. Take a few moments to think about the good things God has done for you. If it was for you personally, write a list of them. If as a group, discuss them with each other.
2. Joshua is passing the baton to the leaders of Israel, but his commission to them is very much like his own commission at the beginning of his leadership. What does this teach us about spiritual battles?
3. Joshua commissions the people to fulfil the task that remains. If you were asked to list three priorities for the church today, what would they be?

Joshua 23:6–16

Looking forward in confidence

Having reminded Israel of what God has done for them, Joshua then reminds the people of their obligations to God and warns them of the consequences of disobedience.

Four commands

At this point, Joshua gives commands which are reminiscent of those God gave to him after the death of Moses (cf. 1:6–9). There are four imperatives. They are to be

- strong (verse 6a);

- submissive (verse 6b);

- separated (verse 7); and

- secure (verse 8).

They are to be strong

The injunction to 'be strong' appears at various times in Scripture (for example, Joshua 10:25; 2 Chronicles 32:7; Isaiah 35:4; Haggai 2:4). We can best understand this in the light of the New Testament exhortations, 'Be strong in the Lord and in his mighty power' (Ephesians 6:10) and 'Be strong in the grace that is in Christ Jesus' (2 Timothy 2:1). This exhortation to be strong is not to make up for deficiency in God but is an expression of confidence in his sufficiency. It is because of who God is, and the confidence they may have in his working on their behalf, that his people may be bold and strong.

They are to be submissive

'Be careful to obey all that is written in the law of Moses, without turning aside to the right or to the left' (verse 6). The law of Moses was the revelation of the mind and will of God. At the beginning of Joshua's leadership he had been told not to let the law depart from his mouth, but to meditate upon it and to do it. Now at the end of his life he passes on the same instruction. The continuity of Israel as the servant of God will be based upon their obedience to the law, the terms of their covenant relationship with him.

They are to be separated

'Do not associate with these nations that remain among you; do not invoke the names of their gods or swear by them' (verse 7). Israel was to stand apart from the nations around them as well as from those remaining within their territory. The attraction of pagan gods was to be a snare that would draw many away in the ensuing years. False gods often appear more attractive than the true God for idols can be tailor-made to our own preferences.

They are to be secure

'You are to hold fast to the LORD your God' (verse 8). No rival to God's position must ever be entertained. There was no question of God not holding fast to them (for example, verse 14b), the only question in the relationship was whether the people would hold fast to him. This principle still applies in our relationship to God.

Separation emphasized

Verses 12 and 13 develop the admonition to separate themselves from the non-Israelite peoples. If they ally themselves with these people or intermarry with them, God will not fulfil his promise to drive out these other nations. There can be no division between God's work and the obedience of the people. Not only will God not drive out the remaining nations, but 'They will become snares and traps for you, whips on your backs and thorns in your eyes, until you perish from this good land which the LORD your God has given you' (verse 13). They, like we after them, may know as much of the Lord fulfilling his word as we really want to. Failure or disaster may come to the people of God but he is never the cause that determined it. It is a case of 'God gave them over . . .' (Romans 1:24, 26, 28). The history of Israel would demonstrate this fact again and again (for example, Judges 3:7–8, 12; 4:1–2; 6:1).

The chapter closes with Joshua summing up his appeal to the leaders (verses 14–16). They know that so far not one of God's promises has failed, every one of them has been fulfilled. But they must not presume upon the faithfulness of God to do them good. God will be equally faithful in bringing all the evil upon them he has threatened, to the extent of even driving them out of the land into which he had brought them, if they violate their covenant with him. God's wrath is as faithful as his love, his anger as consistent as his kindness.

Questions

1. Joshua commands the people to be separated from the non-Israelite nations around them. The command to be separated from the world is given to the church. How do we obey this practically?
2. In the light of God's warning to bring evil on the people if they forsake the covenant with him, how should we under-

stand the discipline of God in Christian experience spoken about in Hebrews 12:5–12, and described as a 'word of encouragement'?

3. How should we apply the note of warning in verses 15–16?

Joshua 24:1–13

A review of God's goodness

The final chapter records Joshua's farewell address to the people of Israel. He traces Israel's history from the call of Abraham to their present dwelling in the land of Canaan.

The final gathering of the Israelites with Joshua took place at Shechem. Significantly, when Abraham migrated from Ur of the Chaldeans to Canaan he came to Shechem and it was there the Lord appeared to him and promised: 'To your offspring I will give this land' (Genesis 12:7). Abraham built an altar to the Lord at Shechem. Now almost 500 years later the promise has come to fruition. For the first time the land is occupied by and belongs to Abraham's offspring.

Jacob had also purchased a piece of ground at Shechem and built an altar there which he called 'El Elohe Israel' (Genesis 33:18–20), which can mean 'God, the God of Israel' or 'Mighty is the God of Israel' (verse 20, NIV footnote). The relationship of that event to this is an obvious one. The nation was able to bear testimony to the greatness of the God of Israel on this site of Jacob's altar, for what followed was an affirmation of God's goodness and power in their experience.

This link with the past is further underlined later in the chapter when Joshua took a large stone and set it up 'under the oak near the holy place of the LORD' (24:26). Mention is made of a 'great tree' at Shechem when God spoke to Abraham about the land (Genesis 12:6), and later Jacob buried the foreign gods his household had collected under the oak at Shechem (Genesis 35:4). The place is described as 'the holy place of the LORD' (Joshua 24:26). We should not take that to mean it was a sacred shrine but it was holy because of its associations with God's dealings with the patriarchs in Israel's past.

Joshua's speech is given as being the words of God himself: 'This is what the LORD, the God of Israel says . . .' (verse 2). In it he narrates God's dealings with Israel from the call of Abraham to the present settlement in the land. The main character in the story is God himself.

'I took your father Abraham . . .' (verse 3)
'I gave him Isaac' (verse 3)
'To Isaac I gave Jacob and Esau' (verse 4)
'I assigned the hill country of Seir to Esau' (verse 4)
'I sent Moses and Aaron' (verse 5)
'I afflicted the Egyptians by what I did' . . . (verse 5)
'I brought your fathers out of Egypt' (verse 6)
'They cried to the LORD for help and he put darkness . . .'
    (verse 7)
'He brought the sea over them and covered them' (verse 7)
'You saw what I did to the Egyptians' (verse 7)
'I brought you to the land of the Amorites' (verse 8)
'I gave them into your hands' (verse 8)
'I destroyed them from before you' (verse 8)
'I delivered you out of his (king of Moab) hands' (verse 10)
'I gave them (citizens of Jericho) into your hands' (verse 11)
'I sent the hornet ahead of you' (verse 12)
'So I gave you a land on which you did not toil' (verse 13)

There were no grounds upon which Israel could congratulate themselves for conquering Canaan. Here was no basis for self-confidence or self-satisfaction. The good things in the five centuries since the story began had all been of God.

God's time-scale

This reminder of the past was no mere academic exercise but crucial to the covenant renewal this was leading towards. As God had been indispensable to their past, so he was indispensable to their future. This was the lesson they had to learn. One of the recurring dangers in history and experience is to forget our complete dependency upon God. Israel's subsequent history reveals their guilt of this despite the warnings given them by Joshua. Christian people have frequently been similarly guilty from New Testament times onwards (for example Galatians 3:3). Joshua teaches us that God is himself indispensable to the accomplishing of his will. He not only reveals his will and gives orders to his people, but he is himself the means of accomplishing it, as he works in co-operation with the obedience of his people to him, and their trust in him.

God indispensable

Another feature of this survey is the length of time it has taken to bring about what God had promised to Abraham. So far, this has only to do with the land itself. The promised 'seed' of Abraham would not arrive until fifteen centuries later. God states of Abraham, 'I gave him Isaac' (verse 3), but it was not fulfilled until 25 years after the promise. He says: 'To Isaac I gave Jacob and Esau' (verse 4), but that took 60 years. Eighty-five years after the promise of Abraham that he would become a great nation through which the world would be blessed, all he has to show for it are twin baby grandsons. He says, 'Jacob and his sons went down to Egypt. Then I sent Moses and Aaron . . .' (verses 4–5), but there is a 400-year gap between those two sentences. We might expect God to work much faster, but he doesn't. Isaiah wrote, 'Woe to those . . . who say, "Let God hurry, let him hasten his work so we may see it" ' (Isaiah 5:19).

God is painting on a bigger canvas than the three-score-years and ten into which we would like everything to fit. There were times in their history when the chosen people of God would almost certainly have given up hope of his promise to Abraham having any real substance. During the years of slavery in Egypt there was not much evidence that these people were destined to bless the world! Many times in their later history they would be brought to the point of despairing that God would ever fulfil his promise – but he did.

The result of God's faithfulness to Israel, now settled in Canaan, was summed up by the Lord: 'So I gave you a land on which you did not toil and cities you did not build; and you live in them and eat from vineyards and olive groves that you did not plant' (verse 13).

Questions

1. Do you think there is value in going back to places or situations where God has revealed himself in particular ways in the past? If so what is the value? Are there any dangers in this?

2. List a few things that we are likely to depend upon in the Christian life as an alternative to God himself. How should we avoid this?

3. God takes his time in developing his story. What are some of the areas in which you find yourself being impatient with God? What should be our attitude in the light of Joshua's record of history?

Joshua 24:14–15

Facing the issues

Now comes the crucial issue. If the people are to fear and serve God they must discard all pagan gods they may have adopted along the way: 'Choose you this day whom you will serve.'

 On the basis of what God has done for them, Joshua challenges the people as to what they must do for God. God's action requires their reaction. His commands require their obedience. His sovereignty requires their humility. His sufficiency requires their dependency. The statement here is reminiscent of Moses' question at the foot of Mount Sinai: 'And now, O Israel, what does the LORD your God ask of you, but to fear the LORD your God, to walk in all his ways, to love him, to serve the LORD your God with all your heart and with all your soul, and to observe the LORD's commands and decrees that I am giving you today for your own good?' (Deuteronomy 10:12–13). Joshua calls for three responses from the Israelites:

'Fear the LORD' (verse 14)

The command 'Do not be afraid' had been given several times in Joshua (for example 8:1; 10:8, 25), but here is the command to 'Fear'. The first time this term occurs in Scripture was after Abraham had taken his son Isaac to Mount Moriah as God had told him, expecting to offer him in sacrifice. As he prepared to strike the fatal blow, the angel of the Lord intervened, 'Now I know that you fear God' (Genesis 22:12). In that context to 'fear God' was to wholly submit to his will irrespective of the consequences. To Abraham the command defied all sense of logic. Not only did he expect to end the life of an innocent boy, but the knife would penetrate and destroy everything God had promised him, for the promise of God to Abraham was wrapped up in his son Isaac. To fear God means not submitting him to the censorship of human rationality. It is unqualified, indiscriminate obedience and it is the cornerstone of a wholesome, healthy relationship with God. Little wonder the writer of Ecclesiastes concludes his book: 'Now all has been heard; here is the conclusion of the matter: Fear God and keep his command-ments, for this is the whole duty of man.' (Ecclesiastes 12:13).

'Serve him with all faithfulness' (verse 14)

The fear of God may be seen as a leaning towards God and service as the practical outworking of that. It is true God had served Israel, as he had earlier reminded them, but they were also to serve God, and to do so faithfully.

'Throw away the gods your forefathers worshipped beyond the River and in Egypt' (verse 14)

The positive command to serve God faithfully has its negative connotations for to serve him is to discard all other gods. Joshua warns them about tolerating that which God has rejected. He mentions the gods from 'beyond the River' (verses 14–15) referring to the Euphrates from which their forefather Abraham came, to the gods of Egypt (verse 14), and the gods of the Amorites (verse 15). In effect he says, 'If you do not wish to serve the Living God then choose whatever god you want. It makes no difference whether they be from the Euphrates, Egypt or from the Amorites for they are equally powerless and equally futile. If a man does not choose to serve the true God, whatever he chooses as a substitute is almost irrelevant for it is doomed to futility.' 'But,' says Joshua, 'As for me and my household, we will serve the LORD' (verse 15).

Questions

1. What are the alternatives to serving God?
2. The statement has been made, 'Fear God and you need fear nothing else'. Do you think this is true? If so, why?
3. Joshua told the people to throw away the gods that their forefathers had worshipped in Egypt. In our own time, what is meant by the statement 'Do not love the world or anything in the world'?

Joshua 24:16–28

Renewing the covenant

In response to the people's positive affirmation of the covenant, Joshua set up a stone as a witness to that act. He then sent the people back to enjoy their tribal inheritance.

The people respond to Joshua with the affirmation that it was the Lord who had brought them from slavery in Egypt and performed great miraculous acts before them; it was he who had protected them along the journey and drove the nations who occupied Canaan, and therefore the issue was settled: 'We too will serve the LORD, because he is our God' (verse 18).

'You cannot serve the Lord'

Joshua's response is a surprising but an important one: 'You are not able to serve the LORD' (verse 19). Some have suggested that this is simply an ancient literary device in which a point is accentuated by making it controversial. (See, for example, Paul P. Enns, *Joshua* (Bible Study Commentary Series, Zondervan, 1981) p. 140.) I do not think so. Surely Joshua is making the point that to rely upon human resolve and resourcefulness as a means of remaining loyal to God is to attempt the impossible. Again and again in the Old and New Testaments and throughout the history of the church God has brought people to a sense of their own inability and of their inherent failure, out of which they have discovered the strength of God by which alone they can do what is required of them. These people have not yet reached that point, for after Joshua tells them that they will turn and serve other gods they reply: 'No! We will serve the LORD' (verse 21). The writer to the Hebrews writes: 'For if Joshua had given them rest, God would not have spoken later about another day . . . for anyone who enters God's rest also rests from his own work, just as God did from his' (Hebrews 4:8–10).

The writer speaks of coming into God's position of rest by ceasing from our own work, something he said Joshua did not lead the people to. The sincerity of the people was admirable in their response to Joshua, but they did not fully understand. It was not long before the Israelites 'forgot the LORD and served the Baals and Asherahs' (Judges 3:7). This refers to the generation Joshua addressed, for as a result God sold Israel into the hands of the king of Aram, and when they cried to God he raised up Othniel, the nephew of Caleb, to rescue them. Othniel was married to Caleb's daughter (see Joshua 15:17) and this event would therefore be within a very short time of Joshua, possibly within five years.

'We will serve the Lord'

Now that they have affirmed their intention, Joshua tells them to 'throw away the foreign gods that are among you and yield your hearts to the LORD, the God of Israel' (verse 23). The link between the false gods and the heart is important to note. Idolatry begins in the heart that is not yielded to God, which is therefore available to whatever appeals to it at the time. The people affirm for the third time: 'We will serve the LORD' (verses 18, 21, 24).

An outward physical sign of their allegiance is now constructed. Joshua recorded these things in a book, and took a large stone and set it under the oak at Shechem as a witness to the words that had been spoken (see comments on 24:1 regarding the significance of placing the oak at Shechem). This is the seventh time a physical memorial has been erected in commemoration of an important event in the book of Joshua: at Gilgal by the Jordan (4:20–24); over Achan's body (7:26); at Ai (8:29); at Mount Ebal (8:30–33); at the cave where the five kings were killed (10:27); at Geliloth by the Jordan (22:10).

Having completed the exercise 'Joshua sent the people away, each to his own inheritance'.

Questions

1. The people give several reasons why they will serve God. Give three reasons why you will serve God.
2. How should we avoid losing the initial sense of dependence upon God that usually characterizes the start of our Christian life (cf. Galatians 3:3; Philippians 1:6; Colossians 2:6–7)?
3. How do you respond to Joshua's statement, 'You are not able to serve the LORD'? Do you accept this verdict about yourself, and if so, how do you then respond to God?

Joshua 24:29-33

Three funerals

The book concludes with the death of Joshua; the final burial of Joseph whose bones had been brought from Egypt; and the burial of Eleazar, Aaron's son, and successor as priest.

Three significant burials

The book of Joshua ends with a record of the burials of three men of importance to Israel's history.

The burial of Joshua

He died at the age of 110 years and was buried in his own town of Timnah Serah amongst his own people of Ephraim. His epitaph is simple: 'Joshua, son of Nun, the servant of the LORD' (verse 29). In these simple words Joshua's life is summed up. History records him as a pioneer and a great national leader, but he would disclaim the initiative that is implied by that. He was simply doing as he was told. Perhaps during his period of leadership there was the greatest evidence of godliness and unity the nation was ever to experience, for under his leadership they had, 'experienced everything the LORD had done for Israel' (verse 31).

The burial of Joseph

As Joseph had requested over 400 years earlier, his bones had been brought from Egypt during the Exodus, carried in the desert for forty years and were now buried in the promised land (Genesis 50:25). They were buried at Shechem on the ground his father had purchased long centuries earlier (Genesis 33:19). This act had great symbolic significance. Joseph knew the day would come when Israel would return to the promised land. Now they were here, settled and at peace. Both Joseph's faith in God, and God's faithfulness to his promises were vindicated by this act.

The burial of Eleazar

Eleazar had been priest since his father Aaron had died during the wilderness years. He had left Egypt as a boy and had witnessed the whole journey to the point of settlement in the land. He would have been less than 20 years on leaving Egypt and therefore not under the curse that had caused all the adult fighting men, except Joshua and Caleb, to die before entering Canaan. He was buried at Gibeah in Ephraim which had been allotted to his son Phineas.

Thus the age and era of Joshua has come to a conclusion. God has demonstrated his faithfulness in returning the people to the land he had intended for them. But it is not the end of the story. Many years, and many generations will pass, and many hardships will be experienced before the ultimate blessing of Israel arrives as a baby in Bethlehem. I am sure the Lord Jesus could have said of Joshua what he said of Abraham, '(He) rejoiced at the thought of seeing my day; he saw it and was glad' (John 8:56).

Questions

1. The epitaph to Joshua in verse 31 gives credit to Israel and credit to God but none to Joshua. Do you know anyone personally of whom something similar would have to be said,

that is, the people around them benefited, and God was seen to be at work? (Compare this with Matthew 5:16.)
2. How do you see the burial of Joseph's bones as a fitting climax to the record of the occupation of the land?
3. In death, Joshua is described as 'the servant of the LORD' (24:29). How do you wish that you will be remembered?

Further reading

Among books that may help readers to explore further are:

Paul P. Enns, *Joshua*, Bible Study Commentary Series (Zondervan, 1981).

Richard Hess, *Joshua*, Tyndale Old Testament Commentaries: (IVP, 1996).

Alan Redpath, *Victorious Christian Living* – Studies in Joshua (Fleming H. Revell, 1994).

Warren Wiersbe, *Joshua: Be Strong* (Scripture Press, 1994).

Martin H. Woudstra, *The Book of Joshua*, New International Commentary (Eerdmans, 1995).

For some interesting and helpful background information:

Werner Keller, *The Bible as History*, Revised edition (Lion and SPCK, 1991).